ROBERT HOLM

Across Ok

With Commentary and Notes by
BILL NAISMITH

METHUEN DRAMA

Methuen Student Edition

This Methuen Student Edition first published in 1994 by
Methuen Drama
an imprint of Reed Consumer Books Limited
Michelin House, 81 Fulham Road, London SW3 6RB
and Auckland, Melbourne, Singapore and Toronto
and distributed in the United States of America by
Heinemann
a division of Reed Elsevier Inc.
361 Hanover Street, Portsmouth, New Hampshire
NH 03901 3959

Across Oka first published in 1988 by Methuen Drama
copyright © 1988, 1994 by Robert Holman
Commentary and Notes copyright © 1994 by Methuen Drama
The author has asserted his moral rights

ISBN 0-413-68320-6

A CIP catalogue record for this book
is available from the British Library

Typeset by Falcon Graphic Art Ltd., Wallington, Surrey
Printed in Great Britain by Cox & Wyman Ltd, Reading, Berks

Contents

References

Throughout the commentary reference is made to immediate critical responses to the plays. These are drawn from the *London Theatre Record*. The relevant volumes are Vol. III No. 10, May 1983 (for *Other Worlds*); Vol. IV No. 22, Nov 1984 (for *Today*); Vol. V No. 11, June 1985 (for *The Overgrown Path*); Vol. VI No. 13, July 1986 (for *Making Noise Quietly*); Vol. VIII No. 9, May 1988 (for *Across Oka*); Vol. X No. 21, Nov 1990 (for *Rafts and Dreams*).

Making Noise Quietly, Today, The Overgrown Path, Other Worlds, Rafts and Dreams and *Outside the Whale* are published by Methuen Drama; *German Skerries* and *Mud* are published by Heinemann (1977); *The Amish Landscape* is published by Penguin Books (1993).

Front cover: Siberian Crane

Production photographs inside the book are of the Royal Shakespeare Company's 1988 production of *Across Oka*. Photographs: Joe Cocks Collection, Shakespeare Centre Library, Statford-upon-Avon.

Thanks are due to Sarah Pia Anderson, Nicholas Barter and Robert Holman for their help and advice in the preparation of this edition.

Robert Holman

Robert Holman was born in 1952 and brought up on a farm in North Yorkshire. On leaving school he worked in a Paddington station bookshop for three years, before being awarded an Arts Council Writer's bursary in 1974. Since then he has spent periods as resident dramatist with the Royal National Theatre and with the Royal Shakespeare Company in Stratford-upon-Avon. His work includes:

1972   *The Grave Lovers*
A one act play, set in a graveyard, about an elderly man looking back with bitter disappointment at some of the events in his life.
Progress in Unity
A show staged in Middlesborough town hall, with eighty teenagers, recounting the history of Cleveland.

1973   *Coal*
A one act play about a group of coal miners, trapped below ground, and their wives waiting to hear news of their safety, or otherwise, on the surface.

1974   *The Nature Cause*
About a young married couple struggling to live in poverty in London, and his schizophrenia.
Mud
Set in North Yorkshire. An old man looks back with bitterness on his life and meets a young couple with everything to look forward to.

1976   *Outside the Whale*
A play, at least in part, about George Orwell and the writer's relationship to his material.

1977   *German Skerries*
A retired teacher meets a young ICI worker in
Middlesborough and they strike up a friendship
that crosses the barriers of culture and age.

1979   *Rooting*
About the people who live and work on a pig
farm, where the action takes place around the
mucking-out of a pig shed.

1980   *The Estuary*
A father and his son spend the night fishing
beside the Tees estuary, when the son learns
about his parents' marriage and their impending
divorce.

Chance of a Lifetime
BBC Television film shown in the 'Play for
Today' strand of dramas about a single parent
father and his two children, one of whom joins
the army and is killed in Northern Ireland.

1983   *Other Worlds*
Set in the eighteenth century, a three-act play
telling the story of how a fishing community
came to hang a monkey, believing it to be a
French spy sent by Napoleon to scout out the
landscape of North East England for a possible
invasion.

1984   *Today*
About a group of people in Yorkshire, one of
whom is a composer, who go to Spain in 1936 to
fight in the International Brigades for the
Republican left-wing cause during the Spanish
Civil War.

1985   *The Overgrown Path*
Set on a Greek island, a young academic arrives
from England to interview an English professor,
now retired and living in seclusion, about his
work on the British hydrogen bomb programme
before and after the Second World War.

Background

The Plays of Robert Holman

Victor An artist can't have politics. He has to be free.
Edward You're behind the times.

Today (p.31)

Robert Holman has written plays in recent years that
have impressed critics and enthused actors and
directors, yet he remains a little apart from the
mainstream of contemporary writers. By concentrating
on the complex emotional lives of ordinary, seemingly
unexciting people he has appeared unfashionable.
Nevertheless, in his distinctive approach to characters,
his concentration on perennial family relationships and
problems, and in his variety of settings, he has presented
an important complementary voice on the English stage.

With many plays in the modern theatre we have little
difficulty in appreciating what they are 'about'. A subject
is chosen by the dramatist and characters serve to
explore that subject. So David Hare's *Racing Demon*
(1990) is clearly about the Church of England and his
Murmuring Judges (1991) is about the law. Both plays can
be seen as commenting on the state of England in the
light of many years of Conservative government.
Likewise, Caryl Churchill's *Top Girls* (1982) is about
post-feminist ambitions in relation to Margaret
Thatcher's advocacy of self-advancement. Sarah Daniels'
Masterpieces (1983) is about pornography. In these and
other like plays 'character' is a function of the play,
serving to advance the argument or dialectic. The
emphasis in Robert Holman's plays is different. He
doesn't write from a conscious view of the world or
engage directly with issues. In his plays people come

first, often drawn from his own personal imaginative experience. It is as convenient for critics as it is for teachers and students to have hooks on which to hang an argument or a meaning. Holman's plays cannot be so neatly summed-up. They are emotional pieces, 'slow, allusive, well-crafted affairs which linger in the mind for weeks rather than making an instant impact' (Colin Shearman, *Guardian*). In support of Holman's approach Benedict Nightingale writes:

> There are playwrights enough – Edward Bond would be the most eminent example – who are only too content to manipulate their audiences along predetermined ideological paths to predestined ideological ends. There's much to be said for writers prepared to stand back, watch, listen and then hand over their tentative discoveries to the audience, leaving it to reach its own conclusions.
>
> *New Statesman* (14.6.85)

The Holman Landscape

> Most people think they live ordinary lives, but nobody's life is ordinary, is it?
>
> *The Amish Landscape* (p.201)

Neil   I want to be ordinary.

> *Rafts and Dreams* (p.83)

In most of Holman's plays the characters are set in a landscape out of doors. This broader natural environment figures as an influence on the characters' mental and emotional lives. The landscape of North Yorkshire, where Robert Holman comes from, is particularly redolent, and the regional Yorkshire idiom is the natural speech of many of his characters. Another Northern artist, L S Lowry, is renowned for his industrial landscapes, peopled by innumerable faceless ordinary folk. Holman focuses in on a minute portion of such a landscape (most often in a rural background), highlighting the individuality and complexity of such ordinariness.

The recurrent theme of Robert Holman's plays is the family. The individual, his family, placed in a real landscape, is the subject of his drama. Characters are shown in relation to or in conflict with their family. They talk about them, or are deeply affected by them. When strangers meet, as often happens, they invariably refer to their family background. Within every family there are different generations, and the sense of generations moving on in time is a driving force in many plays.

Given the nature of the people that Holman chooses to create and write about, the emphasis of the action in his plays is more towards discursive dialogue than outright conflict. Strangers meeting and making contact, sometimes across class barriers, or from different backgrounds, recur in *German Skerries*, *Mud*, the *Making Noise Quietly* trilogy and *The Overgrown Path*. In these and other plays the meeting is often between people from different generations, with different perspectives on life, different questions to ask and insights to offer. This repeated theme has enabled the dramatist to present characters on stage who are older and younger than we are used to seeing, and to give voice to an area of experience largely ignored by our theatre.

Robert Holman has probably written more parts, and certainly more challenging parts, for both mature and young actors than any of his contemporaries. Simply to emphasise the point, from a selection of plays – in *Making Noise Quietly* Sam is 8, May 61 and Helene 57; in *Today* Lucy is 17, Rebecca 8, Elizabeth 61 and Thomas 56; in *Other Worlds* Mary is 14, Peter 12, Anne 54 and Molly 41; in *The Overgrown Path* Mimiko is 16, Clare 12, Beth 69 and Daniel 73. There are, of course, many characters who are younger adults in their twenties and thirties. The age difference between the characters is of

crucial significance in Holman's plays, constantly
forming the very matter of the drama.

Also crucial are the settings in which the characters
are placed. Conventionally we are used to plays that
focus on families being set in a domestic interior
(Ibsen's *A Doll's House*, Miller's *All My Sons*, Osborne's
Look Back in Anger, Pinter's *The Homecoming*). Holman's
plays are invariably set out of doors, in carefully defined
landscapes. There is an obvious practical advantage in
doing this, as it allows strangers to meet accidentally, but
the landscape takes on a greater importance. It is seen
to have a shaping influence, both as part of a character's
history and consciousness, and more directly on the
relationships before us on stage. Ownership of the land
is contested in *Other Worlds*; Matty is seriously affected by
his displacement into the wilds of Oka in *Across Oka*; cast
adrift in the surreal *Rafts and Dreams* the characters are
uniquely able to question their lives. As character is
inevitably shaped by family background, so Holman
believes it is shaped by one's natural environment. Jack
gives voice to this at the end of Scene Two of *German
Skerries*:

Jack Come'n stand where I am.

Carol *goes and stands beside him. They are looking inland.*

Look a'that. A mass of industry. I've never seen it this
time o'the morning before.

A slight pause.

Don't yer get the feelin' yer right in the middle of
somethin'?

A slight pause.

(*pointing from left to right*) The lights o'Redcar. British
Steel. ICI Wilton. Middlesborough. The docks.
Warners Chimney. Teesport refinery. The
Transporter. ICI Billingham. Haverton Hill.

Hartlepool. Stretches f'thirty miles. In the middle of it, we're 'ere. On a jut a'land. Fantastic. (*Shouting very loudly.*) HELLO, HELLO, HELLO. (*After a moment's pause.*) Nobody can 'ear us.

The lights fade.

In many respects *Across Oka* is a typical Holman play. We have representatives of three generations (Jolyon is 74, Tessa 46, Matty 16), and two contrasting families; we have the landscapes of Yorkshire and Russia; we have the meeting of strangers and the detailed probing of their lives; and we have echoes of Holman's key themes – the changing nature of England and English life, pacifism, education and the sense of generations moving on.

The Theatrical Challenge

Robert Holman has attracted an exceptionally loyal following of actors and directors because he has challenged them in the most stimulating ways. The acting in his plays has invariably been recognised by critics as extraordinary, with superlatives abounding – 'luminous', 'utterly truthful', 'mesmerisingly well acted' are typical responses. This is partly a reflection on the meticulous casting of the plays (*Today*, 1984, was actually written for a specific group of actors). It also reflects on the vivid sense of life contained in the dialogue. Most of his work has been commissioned for particular theatres and so, knowing the space for which his plays were being written, Holman conceived them with great empathy for the conditions of performance.

Obviously all actors appreciate good dialogue (a strength of Holman's plays) but his dialogue challenges actors where they are most excited – in creating a fully realised character. This is the consequence of Holman's writing technique, which is akin to how an actor works – he develops characters slowly, instinctively, moving on from what he learns about them, qualifying and even contradicting earlier insights. This is similar to the method explained by Harold Pinter – another dramatist whose focus is on the emotional life of his characters – who had the experience of acting and whose language provides a technical challenge to the performer. Talking of his early work, Pinter claimed:

> I think it is impossible – and certainly for me – to start writing a play from any kind of abstract idea. ... I start writing a play from an image of a situation and a couple of characters involved, and these people always remain for me quite real; if they were not, the play could not be written.
>
> (interview with Kenneth Tynan, BBC Home Service, 28 October, 1960)

The detail with which Robert Holman's characters are filled out, particularly in regard to their family background and history, provides fertile soil for actors' preparation and rehearsal, in keeping with how most of our actors are trained. Stanislavsky's theory of emotion memory requires actors to explore their own living experience in order to find equivalents for the feelings experienced by the characters. All of us can relate to some extent to the family and generation experiences in Holman's plays. Uta Hagen, in *Respect for Acting* (Macmillan, 1973) updates Stanislavsky's 'object exercises' which allow, for example, an actor to re-create two ordinary minutes of life when nothing seems to be happening. Certain questions must be asked: Who am I? What time is it? Where am I? What surrounds me? What are the given circumstances? What is my relationship (to total events, other characters and to things)? What do I want? and so on. In Holman's dialogue, where nothing is surplus, the actor must be confident and *know* why the character says what he does. The research is stimulating.

Holman's awareness of the flaws in human

personality, even in those characters whom he clearly likes, has opened up possibilities for actors that have been rare hitherto. The actress Harriet Walter, for example, writing on *Roles for Women* (New Theatre Quarterly, Vol. IX, No. 34, May 1973) laments the scarcity of roles in the modern theatre that truly reflect women's experience. She claims that the socialist theatre of the 1970's, while 'guilty of marginalising women quite as much as the establishment theatre' limited her to the mimicry of class stereotypes; the new feminists exercised a different stranglehold – their perfectionism 'required us to embody an ideal role model that never wavered from the positive':

> Now I like to think we have come through to a maturity that allows us to be human – that is, imperfect, even if still reaching for perfection, and I want to reflect this on stage. The trouble is that though the feminist consciousness may have come of age, it has not by any means percolated through to the whole of society. I may have given *myself* the licence to be honest, confused, flawed, and human, but the general public does not want it so.

In Robert Holman's plays the truthful awareness of women's imperfection is in balance with women's humanity. Unfortunately, as Harriet Walter concludes, 'too many of (the general public) still want their women portrayed as heroines or harpies'. Holman's women characters are neither, they are real, human and complex.

Holman's external landscapes likewise provide a challenge for the designer. These may be majestic (the vast Oka forest in *Across Oka*) or beautiful (the Greek island of Tinos in *The Overgrown Path*) but they are not pastoral 'escapes' and should not be prettified. All his plays contain lengthy descriptions of settings which require imaginative rather than realistic staging.

Critical Responses

In the absence of more formal academic commentary,
critical response to Robert Holman's work is restricted
to newspaper and journalistic reviews of productions.
These are collated in the *London Theatre Record* (which
includes significant productions outside London). The
major British theatre critics were originally drawn to his
work because it was staged in theatres and by companies
with a reputation for supporting interesting and
innovative new plays and playwrights. In Holman's case
these were The Traverse Theatre, Edinburgh; The Bush
Theatre, London; The Royal Court Theatre, London;
and The Royal Shakespeare Company, Stratford-upon-
Avon and London.

High regard has always been shown for the
production of his plays, and in particular for the acting;
Robert Holman was, from the beginning, recognised for
the quality of his writing and his feeling for character.
Jane Edwardes noted his 'exceptional understanding
and sympathy for his characters' (*Time Out*) as did
Charles Spencer: 'Robert Holman is capable of
spellbinding dialogue and compassionate feeling for the
strength as well as the weakness of human nature'.
(*Evening Standard*) Benedict Nightingale described the
distinctive sound of Holman's voice: 'quiet, rather
gentle, understated, ruminative' (*New Statesman*). The
compelling emotional force of his plays was appreciated:
Andrew Rissick (*Time Out*) found 'a hypnotic emotional
power and complexity' in the plays, and of *Other Worlds*
Barney Bardsley wrote that 'the play is long, measured
and thoughtful, but it holds you to the last minute'
(*Herald Tribune*).

Once Holman was established as a writer to be
seriously regarded, and when his plays took on larger
spaces and greater length, more searching questions
began to be asked concerning dramatic technique and
what Holman really had to say. Michael Billington (who

wrote of *Across Oka* that it is 'an outstanding work that sings with truth') and who believes Holman to be 'a cryptic, oblique dramatist ever reluctant to show his hand', quibbled over *The Overgrown Path*: 'There is nothing wrong with the play's performance – only the riddle-me-ree approach to big ideas. ... The play raises many important moral questions. It also raises vital questions about dramatic technique' (*Guardian*). Benedict Nightingale, though generally reluctant to cavil at Holman's work, sees it at its best 'assured in observation yet diffident when it comes to drawing conclusions' (*New Statesman*). Michael Ratcliffe is not disturbed by this: 'If his full-length plays – *Today, The Overgrown Path* – seldom arrived at the point they were making for, it is because Holman discovers a more interesting subject along the way, usually involving the eye contact of a dialogue for two. That is his forte'. (*Observer*)

The question posed here is whether a dramatist who raises important questions from his observation of human nature is obliged to answer them. Plays are not sermons. Holman follows the ambiguities in his characters and these do not lead to neat conclusions or suggest any simplistic path to a perfect world.

Synopsis

Act One, Scene One

The setting is the cobbled backyard of a small terraced house in Middlesborough, Yorkshire, in 1986. Jolyon (Jolly), soon to be joined by his wife Eileen, is talking to his sixteen-year-old grandson Matty. He recalls how, many years ago, his best friend Aram Kabalevsky returned to Russia and sent him a present of two Siberian Crane eggs. He has been reminded of them by a television programme which told of how a Russian ornithologist (also called Kabalevsky) is hoping to revive the endangered species by returning some live eggs to Russia from a bird sanctuary in North America. The coincidence of the names has prompted Jolyon to write to the BBC, seeking further information. Jolyon now gives his own egg shells to Matty. Jolyon has a longing to visit Russia, but Eileen thinks this is an unrealistic and irresponsible idea. Jolly hopes to finance a visit by selling his boat, and he invites Matty to help him paint it. Jolly and Matty exchange confidences when alone. They are joined by Tessa – Matty's mother – and Jolly is drawn to reminisce about the harsh domestic circumstances of his and Eileen's early married life.

Act One, Scene Two

A month later, and Jolly has just died. Eileen is left with conflicting emotions. She remembers Jolly as a dreamer, embittered by his working-class background. She feels guilty about stifling him and resentful that Tessa's education and progress as a doctor have distanced her.

Act One, Scene Three

Later that day Matty and a 'ghostly' Jolyon are painting
the boat on a shingle beach. Jolyon disappears and
Matty is joined by his mother, Tessa. He shows her
Jolly's store of food supplies which he has been keeping
in the boat for his imagined trip to Russia. Tessa
interprets this as Jolly's perverse means of coping with
the forceful Eileen. Upset by her father's death and
worried about her mother, the exhausted Tessa begins
to find fault with Matty.

Act One, Scene Four

Outside Tees Sailing Club, where Jolly's boat is up for
sale, Matty, Eileen and Tessa are preparing for a picnic
when they are joined by Professor Pavel Kabalevsky,
director of the Oka nature reserve in Russia. He has
come in response to Jolyon's letter to the BBC. He
explains his proposed visit to America to reclaim some
crane eggs. At first his presence disturbs Eileen, but he
joins the picnic and talks of his family – his English wife
Margaret and his fourteen-year-old son Nikolai. Pavel
thinks it might be possible for him to arrange for Matty
to visit his family in Russia and see the White Siberian
Crane.

Act One, Scene Five

In Tessa's expansive garden, Eileen, still grieving for
Jolyon, is in a confused emotional state ('I expect I've
got everything jumbled up'). She expresses her sense of
personal failure and her worries about Matty being
favoured in life. She is jealous of his proposed visit to
Russia. Tessa encourages her to think positively of the
future.

Act Two, Scene One

The action moves to the village of Brukin Bor in Russia, eight months later. Margaret greets Matty and Eileen who have travelled by train and bus from Moscow. They have been met by Nikolai. Margaret fills out her family history for Eileen, telling her of her Quaker and pacifist background in Tunbridge Wells, her headmaster father, teacher training in Cambridge, her meeting with Pavel and her two older children who are living and working away. Eileen is responding to the new insights which she is experiencing, being so far from home. Nikolai is very excited about the visitors and the prospect of his father bringing the White Crane to Oka.

Act Two, Scene Two

At night Matty and Nikolai are preparing for bed in Pavel's small office when he returns with three White Crane eggs in a portable incubator. One has died, the other two are fertile. Pavel explains how carefully they must be looked after. Despite Margaret's apprehension he leaves the eggs in the boys' safekeeping overnight. There is a strong focus on the eggs during this scene, but it is important to appreciate how differently the boys are treated by the adults in this and the following scene.

Act Two, Scene Three

Two days later the boys are getting ready to take the eggs to the Oka forest to plant them in a nest of a Grey Crane. Pavel is confident that Nikolai and Matty can be trusted with them.

Act Two, Scene Four

The boys are in the Oka forest at the point where they must leave their boat. Matty becomes intensely irritated by the younger Nikolai's superior technical knowledge, his incessant questioning and the fundamental inability of the two to properly understand each other.

Act Two, Scene Five

Deeper in the forest the boys find the Grey Crane's nest and begin the process of transferring the eggs. There is still a friction between them and when Nikolai refuses Matty's desperate plea for recognition Matty hits the two live eggs together and destroys them. Some awareness of a mutual responsibility effects a reconciliation.

Commentary

Form and Meaning

Jolyon I like patterns, you know. I always look for the pattern in a thing.

Across Oka (p.18)

Daniel How much d'you ever know the consequences of something which isn't yet finished? The pattern comes later.

The Overgrown Path (p.175)

Martin The world isn't a rational place. Things aren't changed by rational people.

German Skerries (p.55)

Of the ten sequential scenes in *Across Oka* the first five (Act One) take place in England and the second five (Act Two) take place in Russia. This even division invites the conclusion that the play is concerned to an extent with a comparison of the two countries. According to Michael Billington, the play 'perfectly fuses symbol and reality, exposing the strengths and limitations of two opposed political philosophies' showing that 'the cherished freedom of the West carries a destructive capacity, while the imposed order of the East crushes something in the spirit' (*Guardian*). This is echoed by Michael Ratcliffe in his summing-up:

> *Across Oka* is about metamorphosis and manipulation in the lives of passionate, gentle people in North Yorkshire and Western Siberia (*sic*), the first open to all experience, the second constrained by the discipline of an enclosing state.
>
> (*Observer*)

The trouble with these views is the implication that the two different families – the English Davises and the Russian Kabalevskys – and more particularly the two boys, Matty and Nikolai, are constructed as 'representative' of different cultures, and that the play's main concern is with these cultures and political systems. A close consideration of the two families, however, reveals that they are too distinctive to be fully representative.

The families and the boys are indeed products of their backgrounds but they are a complex mix. For example, Margaret was born English and the Russian Nikolai speaks English better than his teacher; Matty goes to an established English public school whereas Eileen is inhibited by her lack of formal education. In performance the key to each scene lies in its emotional content, which suggests that the dramatist's concern is with the characters and their relationships. Nevertheless various themes and metaphorical ideas are contained within the play. An alternative view of the play's structure is offered by Lyn Gardner:

> Holman's play is constructed like a Russian doll in reverse – the removal of each layer revealing a larger theme, a broader canvas, greater ambition.
>
> (*City Limits*)

The play has a strong narrative line which links each scene without obtruding unduly. This concerns the story of the White Crane's eggs. Jolyon initiates the action by writing to the BBC, following a television programme mentioning the eggs and Kabalevsky. Pavel follows this up after Jolyon's death and invites Matty to his home at Oka in Russia. Matty travels there with Eileen. When Pavel arrives back from America with two live crane's eggs he allows Matty and Nikolai to take them into the forest where Matty breaks them in an uncontrolled fit of pique. This action is shocking and surprising in performance but there is a degree of inevitability about it. It is, perhaps, the only possible conclusion of the action initiated by Jolyon when we consider the characters involved. The RSC production underlined this inevitability by having the character Jolyon place the Grey Crane's nest on stage before the last scene.

Jolyon enjoys connections in life – 'I like patterns, you know. I always look for a pattern in a thing' (p.18). There are several intriguing coincidences and connections in the play, beginning with the two Kabalevskys. They have the same name, a common interest in crane's eggs, but are not related. Jolyon harbours two dead crane's eggs and the memory of two stillborn children; his actions lead to the abortion of two more eggs at the end of the play. He remembers being woken at night, when in his brother's pyjamas, by a Russian carrying two eggs; Matty and Nikolai are not in their rightful pyjamas at night when a Russian brings two eggs to them. Jolyon and Pavel are both described as 'dreamers'. As the White Siberian Crane has become displaced, so Matty undergoes a profound displacement – away from all security. These coincidences, whether consciously or unconsciously included in the play, echo the unpredictability of coincidence in real life. While generally showing concern for individual responsibility and an aversion for those who manipulate others, Robert Holman occasionally introduces in his work a freak event suggesting the limitations of human achievement (lightning kills Sarah in *The Overgrown Path* and a bomb falls on Harry in *The Amish Landscape*).

Across Oka is much concerned with death at the beginning – deaths in Jolyon's family and his own death; and towards the end of the play the precious crane's eggs are killed. But the ending is not altogether depressing. The force of the action suggests life going on, and is, finally, affirmative and hopeful.

The White Crane

Pavel I dream of the day I see the White Siberian Crane.

Across Oka (p.45)

Nikolai We shall have the White Crane at Oka?

Across Oka (p.88)

It is important to place the dramatic significance of the White Crane in the play, and in particular the White Crane's eggs. At one extreme they have been taken very seriously, as the *raison d'être* of the story. The play has been described as 'a small-scale ecological tragedy' (Michael Coveney, *Financial Times*). There is no doubt that in performances by The Royal Shakespeare Company (1988) and The Royal Academy Of Dramatic Art (1993) the breaking of the eggs by Matty in the last scene produced anguished responses from audiences – gasps and tears were not uncommon. The act is appalling and shocking. The embryos are killed. But the action does not portend the end of the world. It does not even portend the end of the White Crane. When asked by Eileen 'what happens if there aren't any fertile eggs?', Margaret replies 'My husband will try again next year'.

The eggs gain significance in performance because of the care and attention that is paid to them on stage. They are regarded as precious objects. In production added significance has been applied to them circumstantially. At RADA the production opened with a filmed projection of the White Crane in flight, accompanied by a hauntingly beautiful cor anglais solo. The natural beauty of the bird was given maximum emotional impact. Later, when Pavel entered with the eggs (Act Two, Scene Two) lighting focused on the incubator with a powerful effect. The RSC production programme contained only two pieces of information apart from crediting actors, the production team and the company – a design for making a paper crane and details of the bird's symbolic associations:

> In Japan, the crane has always been a symbol of long life and good fortune, its graceful long-necked form appearing in textile designs and woodblock prints over the centuries. It is also one of the most popular figures found in books on origami, where instructions for folding paper cranes go back hundreds of years. More recently, though, the folded paper crane has achieved a new and wider significance, as a symbol of international peace. This began with a little Japanese girl, Sadako Sasaki, a victim of the Hiroshima bomb who, as she lay in hospital, folded cranes from the paper her medicine was wrapped in. Her goal was to fold a thousand cranes, in the hope that if she did, her prayers for recovery would be answered. When she eventually realised that there would be no recovery for her, she began to pray instead for universal peace. Sadako managed to complete 644 cranes; after her death, the remaining number were made up by other children and then, as the story spread throughout Japan, children from all over the country began to send paper cranes to Hiroshima as symbolic prayers for peace.

For many members of the audience the quality of acting in performances of *Across Oka* persuaded them that the eggs were real, and the breaking of the eggs was a real event. The eggs were, of course, stage props and not real at all. In contrast, the BBC World Service radio recording of the play reduced the dramatic impact of the eggs considerably. Their visual dimension and the physical relationship with them (handling, carrying etc.) – which on stage accorded them almost the role of a character – counted far less.

The crane's eggs are in fact dramatic props, significant in so far as they provide for the narrative line.

Matty and Eileen go to Russia because Pavel has been drawn to their Yorkshire home by Jolly's letter concerning his crane's eggs. The play is then concerned more with what happens to Matty when he is displaced into the wilds of the Oka reserve with Nikolai.

The eggs are precious objects, which should be returned to their natural habitat, but they are not symbolic. They are real in the play world. They are very important to Pavel: 'This is what I have striven for, for ten years', 'The pinnacle of our life here is Pavel's work with the cranes'. They don't carry the symbolic significance of the cherry orchard in Chekhov's play or the wild duck in Ibsen's play. They have more of a metaphorical significance. Our real concern should be with why they are broken and what is happening between Matty and Nikolai. In this respect they are more closely akin to the baby in Edward Bond's *Saved* (1965) who is killed by a gang of youths. This act is also appalling and shocking but the dramatic significance of the act is to make us relate to the baby as a victim of human inadequacy. Similarly we should focus on Matty and Nikolai and ask why the eggs are broken.

Family Relationships

Tessa My problems, Matty's problems, they're not of your making. Are they?

Eileen No. Why do I feel so guilty then?

Across Oka (p.58)

Matty We're a funny family.

Across Oka (p.31)

All the characters in *Across Oka* are so strongly identified through their family relationships that the family might be considered the true subject of the play. The complexity of Holman's plays has much to do with the

difficulties his characters experience in coming to terms
with their lives and their families. This is especially true
of the English family in *Across Oka*. Matty's question to
his mother, Tessa, about her mother, Eileen – 'You
don't like her very much do you, Mum?' – is, for her,
manifestly unanswerable. One view of the play, though
as we have seen, not the only one, is that it tells Matty's
story. Matty's progress through the play is determined by
how his family has evolved through generations.

Act One is a beautifully crafted description of family
relationships; of what holds a family together, and what
tensions and frustrations can exist within it. Through
reminiscence Jolyon, and later Eileen, vividly portray an
early married life in the 1930's urban Yorkshire working
class. Though temperamentally incompatible and forced
into marriage by pregnancy, the two were held together
by children and a fierce family pride. A subtly
discriminating class system dominated, insisted on, and
maintained certain standards of living. It was necessary
to show a family solidarity and a quality to the 'outside'
world – defined in the play as 'the street'. The details
sound more like fact than fiction:

> **Jolyon** We moved here when your mum was four and
> Stephen was two. It was a step up for us then. The
> neighbours were really stand-offish and snooty,
> thinking yer gran was common. She cleaned this
> house from top to bottom with yer mum and Stephen
> hanging on to her pinny.
>
> (p.19)

Eileen has the same puritanical instinct almost fifty years
later, when Jolly dies: 'I'll wash 'im, lay 'im out. I don't
want the undertaker thinking anything of us'. This urge
for a decent family reputation produced friction
indoors. When Eileen says: 'All my life I've been in the
middle of battles. . . . Battles to keep our head above
water' she is remembering her marital strife with the

impractical and romantically inclined Jolly; 'I used to think: we'll not have a family if I let him dream – we'll be out on the streets – we'll be begging.' At times she could be 'particularly savage' towards him. These domestic battles, and the shared crises, including the accidental death of the son, Stephen, forged a marriage. The partnership has been uneasy, and the early scenes suggest an ongoing friction, but Jolyon is finally able to answer Matty:

Matty But you learnt to love her, didn't you?

Jolyon I think so. Yes.

(p.27)

Their daughter Tessa's educational advancement to the status of doctor ('You've made your life very good') is a mixed family blessing. The source of family pride, especially to Jolyon, Tessa has been educated out of her class and has moved away. The play eloquently and movingly distinguishes the difference between the daughter/father and the daughter/mother relationship, the first being much closer, warmer and direct.

The grandson Matty is placed in a prestigious school as a fee-paying boarder. This is a sign of further social and material advancement: the school 'positively drips with well-being', and is far removed from anything Jolyon or Eileen could have experienced. However Matty is not, at sixteen, completely at ease. He is accused by Tessa of becoming a manipulator, but in the play we see him being manipulated. He is sensitive and good natured but has problems communicating with the older generations. In his case it might well be asked: 'When did you last see your father?' because the missing father is a powerful absence in his life and in the play. There are many plays where the dead or absent father features strongly (for example, *Hamlet*, Ibsen's *Ghosts*, Lorca's *The House of Bernada Alba*, Tennessee Williams's

The Glass Menagerie) as we focus on what they have left behind. Matty's father has emigrated to America but essentially he does not exist. This is surely an important factor in Matty's character. The presence of Pavel in Act Two serves to highlight the absence of a father figure. Tessa has become 'cocooned' from Matty and the play reveals that nobody knows him very well or listens to him very much. His deep rooted problem of identity explodes at the end of the play.

Nikolai differs from Matty in that his life is completely determined by family and social orthodoxy. He is constantly being told by his mother what he can and can't do. He wears the red scarf of the Young Pioneers which symbolises his commitment to the basic tenets of Communist society, and to social obedience. He is used to doing things with and for other people; independence is an unknown concept. He understands the parameters of his world and is secure within them. Matty has greater material advantages, but not such security:

> **Jolyon** Are you wanting to be told off?
>
> **Matty** I'm not saying that. Actually, I wouldn't mind occasionally.

(p.14)

Also Nikolai, though young and immature, is part of a loving family. His parents are closely united by a shared social ideology, a shared concern for Pavel's work on the nature reserve and a mutual attraction:

> **Eileen** We didn't fall in love like that. It's good to see a woman who doesn't have regrets. You don't, do you?
>
> **Margaret** No.

(p.69)

Communication

Matty Most boys feel their families don't really listen to them.

Across Oka (p.14)

Eileen If I was him sitting here you'd be telling him the truth, wouldn't you? I've always kept the truth away.

Across Oka (p.26)

For a play that concentrates on intimate conversation it is ironic that *Across Oka* draws so much attention to the difficulties of communication, particularly between family members. There is a profound psychological realism in the depiction of different codes of speech between different generations, sexes and nationalities. The theme lies at the heart of the last two scenes where a complete breakdown in communication between Matty and Nikolai precipitates the devastating breaking of the crane's eggs.

The opening scene ostensibly introduces details of Kabalevsky and the White Siberian Crane – a conventional exposition. Immediately, however, we are made aware of the subtle and complex verbal strategies that are being employed by the family. Jolly teases Matty: 'Jolly do stop it, it isn't fair', and annoys Eileen with talk of going to Russia. Eileen shows her frustration: 'You're an old bugger, Jolyon. Stop it', and is quick to reprimand Matty: 'I think you can be too hard on a small child, Matty'. Matty, meanwhile, is being polite. The grandparents 'use' Matty as the third person rather than speak directly to each other. There is, however, a subtext to all this, which emerges as Jolly's incontinence – a source of bitterness, embarrassment and concern to them both. Jolyon confides this to Matty, as he has previously done to Tessa by secretly visiting her hospital. His secrecy extends to collecting a store of provisions in his boat for an improbable escape. It appears that even within the intimacy of the family group certain things cannot be said or acknowledged. Not until Act Two do we learn that the marriage was set up by Eileen in a way that Jolyon never knew: 'I married Jolly to get away from my mother. ... It was easy you see because I told Jolly I was pregnant by him. In actual fact it was another boy.' (p.41)

Matty's situation as son and grandson is somewhat invidious, as he is well aware. He talks (but only to his grandfather) of his 'problem with Mum' and admits that 'Most boys feel their families don't really listen to them. Or know them.' In a revealing, but unhelpful, exchange Jolly asks:

> **Jolyon** D'you think yer Gran an' me don't listen to you?
>
> *A slight pause.*
>
> **Matty** No.
> **Jolyon** What a liar.
> **Matty** Liar?
> **Jolyon** Yes. Liar.
>
> *A slight pause.*
>
> **Matty** You leave me no option but to say 'yes' then.
> **Jolyon** True?
> **Matty** It might not be true. I don't know, Grandpa.
>
> (pp.14/15)

Matty's 'problem with Mum' emerges in the scenes following Jolyon's death, when grief releases inhibitions in Eileen and Tessa and tension causes Matty to have a hard time. 'Don't patronise me' and 'don't get at me' are his response to his mother, while Eileen sharply admonishes him: 'You're far too quick to jump on money.'

The relationship between Eileen and Tessa, mother and daughter, is presented with acute psychological awareness of the tensions involved. Only the crisis of Jolyon's death allows the unspoken to be aired between two who are 'so much at cross-purposes'. The love and the caring which is endemic within this family is heartfelt but not without its strains.

The Russian family adds another dimension to the theme of communication. Everything seems more straightforward and psychologically uncomplicated between these family members. Margaret, who is fifty-four and has two older children, imposes a strict regime on the young Nikolai knowing that he has advantages. Nevertheless Nikolai is secure in the knowledge of his family's love and protection. Act Two dramatises the effect on Eileen and Matty of their journey into the unknown. Eileen grows in self-awareness, but Matty is exposed to a family and a culture that proves very disturbing.

The climax of the play is reached in the final two scenes when the boys are alone in the Oka forest. Matty has observed the close physical intimacy between the Russian family, the fondling of Nikolai, and his father's close concern and attention for him and his trust in him. The brief Scene Three of Act Two highlights the family warmth and affection. The effect is to make Matty feel excluded and insecure. When removed to the forest with the younger Nikolai he wants to be recognised and in charge. He fails, partly because he does not have the technical expertise of Nikolai, but more crucially because Nikolai does not understand his need.

Nikolai has lived entirely in the knowledge that you must do things with other people and for other people; he cannot see the individual problem being experienced by Matty. He literally does not understand:

Matty You're hurting me, Nikolai.
Nikolai Please, Matty, tell me why I'm hurting you?

A slight pause.

Matty It's particularly difficult because you haven't done anything wrong.

A slight pause.

Nikolai I don't understand. Matty, I must know.
Matty It's not you, you idiot. It's me.
Nikolai Pardon?
Matty It's me.

A slight pause.

Nikolai Pardon?

(p.108)

The irony of this conflict is that Nikolai is the first person in the play who attempts to listen to Matty. His direct and personal criticism of Matty has a deep effect:

Nikolai I think you are a boy who always feels sorry for himself, Matty.
Matty (*gently*) Do I?
Nikolai Yes, you do.

A slight pause

Matty Do I seem self-pitying?
Nikolai Yes.

(p.112)

When Nikolai fails to respond to Matty's pleading the eggs get broken, more by accident than intent. Matty loses control. However the experience develops Matty's character. For the first time in the play he says 'No' (when Nikolai suggests lying), and he shows that he is prepared to take responsibility for what has happened.

Education

Martin Teach your children to ignore their sense of

responsibility. Teach them to love you. They're not the same thing.

German Skerries (p.24)

The need for education to keep in touch with changing times, and its vital importance for the individual is a constant theme in Holman's work.

Education, both in the formal sense of institutional learning, and more broadly as an aspect of how we learn about life, is a recurrent motif in *Across Oka*. Jolyon is fundamentally an educated man ('He washed his hands before opening a book did Jolly') although he could not afford to study. When Tessa went to university 'he shone like the sun'. Eileen admits to being jealous of their intelligence, but this is a complex psychological reaction to her experience. She feels ignorant, but clearly she isn't, and also she knows she isn't. As she says: 'I can't help it. It's the way I was brought up'.

Matty and Nikolai's experience of education is very different as we have seen. Margaret explains her upbringing in Act Two, Scene One, and both she and Pavel place a high priority on Nikolai's education. Margaret has something of the zeal of the convert, holding very definite views about society and justice. She is akin to the pacifist John Bell in Holman's novel *The Amish Landscape* who joins the Amish community in Pennsylvania out of religious commitment. He knows he will never be a complete Amishman, but he is satisfied that his children are fully integrated among the Amish. Margaret worries about Nikolai being pushed too hard by his father – but then all the mothers in the play worry about their children.

Time and Place

Admiring Robert Holman's gift for characterisation, Michael Coveney claims that his 'ability to suggest a "life lived" is rooted in a detailed account of a character's background' (*Financial Times*). The reminiscence in *Across Oka*, particularly of the older characters Jolyon, Eileen and Margaret serve a double purpose. They provide a realistic social context for the characters on stage. We know exactly where they have all come from. But of equal dramatic significance is the fact that these histories are placed alongside the lives of younger generations, represented by Tessa and most notably Matty and Nikolai. The effect is to convey the passing of time, to recognise that times change and that generations move on. The play is no more judgmental about this than it is about the contrasting social systems of England and Russia: time passing and society changing is part of the 'natural way of things'.

Details of the past go back to the First World War. Margaret explains her family's pacifism deriving from their experience: 'My grandfather was shot in the Great War, by a firing squad, for refusing to fight.' She goes on to recount a pleasant middle-class home counties life which included 'teas on the lawn, and lemonade' and the 'run to Brighton in the car'. She explains how her move to Russia was difficult and how 'It still isn't easy to be completely accepted'. But now, even in Russia, under the repeals introduced by President Gorbachev in the 1980's, things are changing:

> Nikolai is growing up with all this excitement surrounding him, so it's rather different. Edvard and Rafiya didn't see their father travelling abroad.
>
> (p.67)

The ability and freedom to travel is the major distinction Pavel makes between the East and West.

The progress of the English family during the century is essentially one of material advancement. The hardship and poverty of Jolyon and Eileen's early married life is vividly described in the early scenes: 'I don't wish what

we went through on anybody' says Eileen. The naming
of people and places brings the past alive – Scarborough,
Linthorpe Grange, Mrs Colling, Bolckow Street with its
damp, where 'Mr Troop battered their Keith'. Their
circumstances have, however, changed with time. Once,
a television was unthinkable; later 'They viewed the
world from the television'. Matty's material advantages
are very evident, both in the description of his school
and when he goes to Russia: 'Nikolai's anorak is not as
bright, and is a much poorer quality than Matty's'.
Eileen is apprehensive about people 'having more',
believing that it creates more responsibility and 'the
more people have, the less responsible they are'.

Eileen displays a worldly wisdom aphoristically
throughout the play – 'There is a price for whatever we
do', 'children are miracles', 'It's easier to think the right
thoughts than it is to do the right things' – which points
to a common human experience, regardless of place
and time. But her history, like that of all the other
characters, is one of coming to terms with changing
circumstances.

The Play in Performance

As with all plays, performance adds another dimension
to the 'dramatic text' – that is the 'literary' text, as
contained in this volume. *Across Oka* is typical of Robert
Holman's plays in that it reads very well, and the
characters and settings are described in considerable
detail. However the literary text is essentially a blueprint
for production and contains the potential for live
performance. The humour, warmth and wit of the play
comes across better in performance, but primarily the
responsibility of the actors is to communicate the depth
of emotion felt by the characters and to evoke the
feeling generated between them.

The play is technically demanding of the actor in that the writing is 'on the line' and the acting must be 'on the line' also. This demands respect for Holman's style. In tennis, when the ball is played from the base line we tend to get good rallies and a good rapport between players: when the players are not on the line the action is all over the place. Actors have to fit in with the thought pattern of the people on stage and know *why* they are saying things, because nothing is given to the audience by way of anticipation. Words have to be played for the sincerity of the meaning, without false nuance or colouring. The thought is in the punctuation, not in the line. The energy is in the line. Consider, for example, the end of Scene Two when the bereaved Eileen is talking to Tessa. The simplicity of the lines and the vocabulary belie the weight of emotion that is represented and which is communicated only when the full context is appreciated by the actors:

Eileen I used to think: we'll not have a family if I let him dream – we'll be out on the streets – we'll be begging. Isn't that stupid? I'm sorry, Tess.
Tessa It isn't stupid, Mum.
Eileen It is, you know.

A slight pause.

I suppose the one thing I've learnt – is that somehow you do get by. That must be true, because we did.
Tessa Yes.
Eileen I am sorry.
Tessa You've nothing to be sorry for.
Eileen I have, you know.

A slight pause.

Tessa It's Dr Cottie, isn't it Mum?
Eileen Mmm?
Tessa Your doctor. Dr Cottie?
Eileen Yes, it is.

(p.26)

The effect, when actors trust the language and recognise how far each line leads to the next, is to convey the powerful emotional content convincingly.

From this it might be deduced that the play and the style do not invite or encourage distracting physical action. The play is relatively still. Holman gives stage directions when he considers movement to be necessary – and it is worth considering these when reading the text.

The play does invite a close, attentive audience and a relatively intimate space for performance. It is essential for actors to appreciate a sense of place if atmosphere is to be created. In each scene certain characters are on 'home' ground, others are not. This awareness of a strong social reality is helped in performance by costume, and Holman defines costume in the text.

Productions of *Across Oka* have tended to include music (originally composed) as a scenic link, or as a further pointer to social background. It is useful to consider what music is appropriate. The words 'gentle' and 'heartfelt', often applied to Holman's plays, might lead to a false sense of poetic beauty. The plays, including *Across Oka*, are quite tough in their depth of observation of human nature and a false note of lyrical beauty in the musical accompaniment would be wrong.

Act One, Scene One   (p.8)
Matty and Jolyon

Act One, Scene Three (p.29)
Matty and Tessa

Act One, Scene Four (p.52)
Eileen and Pavel

Act One, Scene Five (p.56)
Eileen and Tessa

Act Two, Scene One (p.62)
Margaret, Matty and Eileen

Act Two, Scene Two (p.92)
Nikolai, Pavel and Matty

Act Two, Scene Three (p.96)
Margaret, Pavel, Matty and Nikolai

Act Two, Scene Five (p.112)
Nikolai and Matty

Across Oka

This edition is dedicated to the memory of
Patricia Lawrence and Richard Haddon Haines

Across Oka was first performed by the Royal Shakespeare Company at the Other Place, Stratford-upon-Avon on 13 April 1988. The cast was as follows:

Jolyon	Alfred Burke
Matty	Edward Rawle-Hicks
Eileen	Patricia Lawrence
Tessa	Jane Cox
Pavel	Richard Haddon Haines
Margaret	Joan Blackham
Nikolai	Timothy Stark

Directed by Sarah Pia Anderson
Designed by Ashley Martin-Davis

The play is set in the summer of 1986 and the spring of 1987.

Act One

Scene One

The cobbled backyard of a small terraced house. A warm July afternoon.

The four sides of the yard incline slightly towards the centre where there is a drain covered by a metal grid. Two wooden kitchen chairs are set apart from one another. On one of them is a lace-making board with some lace in progress, and on the ground is a newspaper which is open at the crossword, a dictionary, and a biro.

Jolyon *is sitting in the other chair. There is his cardigan draped over the back, and on the ground is a library book. On his lap is a wooden box in a plastic Boots carrier bag.*

Jolyon *is a tall, thin, dignified man of seventy-four, with a shock of white hair. He is wearing socks, sandals, trousers, and a shirt with the sleeves rolled to the elbow.*

Matty *is standing beside him.*

Matty *is a young, fresh-faced, fair-haired boy of sixteen. He is cleanly dressed in good trainers, jeans, and a t-shirt. He is wearing an expensive wristwatch.*

Jolyon Aram Kabalevsky was my best friend. We were both eight. His parents were refugees from Tsarist old Russia, although he was born here. I remember saying to Aram: how can you return when you've never been there? He said: my dad knows Vladimir Ilyich Lenin, and we're going.

A slight pause.

A year later I was in bed, Matty, when my mother called up the stairs. I can still hear her voice. I came down in my brother's pyjamas and there was a gentleman on the doorstep. My mother said: this gentleman's Russian,

Jolly. He said: was I Jolyon Davis, he had a present from my best friend who'd returned to the Soviet Union.

He takes the box from the carrier bag. It is roughly made and was nailed together many years ago by a child.

It was this. With it was a letter from Aram which I must've lost. I tried writing back to the address, but nothing ever happened. I think eventually the post office decided it was impossible to write to Russia. My friend had disappeared again.

Eileen *enters from the house. She is carrying a small plate on which is a slice of fruit-cake.*

Eileen *is a thin woman of seventy. Her hair is neatly done. She is wearing a short-sleeved cotton dress, stockings, and stoutish shoes.*

Eileen *takes the plate to* **Matty**.

Eileen It's lovely to see you.

Jolyon Of course it is.

Eileen Don't wait to be asked.

Matty *smiles, he begins to eat the cake.*

Eileen *goes to her chair and sits down. She picks up the lace-making board, but she doesn't work at it.*

Jolyon A month ago we were watching a wildlife programme on the television. It was mostly about the Siberian Crane, which is now almost extinct in Russia. It's been pillaged and its habitats have been destroyed. In America – where was it?

Eileen A place called the International Crane Foundation, in Wisconsin.

Jolyon In Wisconsin they're now breeding these Siberian Cranes. They've taken some eggs from the very north of Siberia, hatched them in America, and now they're hoping to take some eggs from those birds back to Russia, and put them back into the wild.

Matty I think I saw it.

Eileen Have you got a television at school?

Matty We have occasionally.

Jolyon It wouldn't mean anything t'you, but the Russian ornithologist in the programme was called Professor Pavel Kabalevsky. Can you guess what Aram Kabalevsky's present was all those years ago?

Eileen Don't tease him.

Matty What?

Jolyon Have a guess.

He taps the box.

What's in here?

Eileen Jolyon.

Matty I don't know, it could be anything.

Jolyon It couldn't you know.

Eileen Don't encourage 'im, Matty.

Matty A bomb. Or something.

Eileen He wants you to make a fool of yourself.

Jolyon I don't.

Jolyon *taps the box.*

Matty You're succeeding, Grandpa.

Jolyon Think about what I've told you.

A slight pause.

Eileen Jolly, do stop it, it isn't fair. Let him eat his cake in peace.

Jolyon *lifts the lid from the box.*

Matty Eggs.

Jolyon Not just any eggs.

Matty What? Siberian Crane eggs? Really?

Jolyon Yes.

Matty Wow.

The two eggs are nestled in two recesses within the box.

Matty *kneels to look more closely.*

Where did he get them from?

Jolyon Siberia, I suppose. We collected eggs. Many boys did.

Matty Why haven't I seen them before?

Jolyon They've been tucked away in the loft.

Matty I hate to say it, Jolly, but this is probably why they're extinct.

Jolyon I know.

Matty Your friend didn't seem to care terribly much.

Eileen I think you can be too hard on a small child, Matty. Especially then.

Matty *finishes his cake.*

Matty What are you going to do with them?

Jolyon Nothing.

Matty *takes an egg from the box.*

Matty May I have one of them?

Jolyon No. Not yet.

Matty *holds the egg up to the sun.*

I wondered if there was a connection. What do you think?

Matty I don't know.

Eileen If you tell him there is, you'll make his year.

Jolyon It's the two names. Kabalevsky.

Eileen Jolly. Honestly.

Jolyon I think it's possible. What d'you think?

Matty Why don't you write to the BBC? Or something.

Eileen He has already. He sits by the letterbox every morning as if it was his birthday.

Jolyon I'd like us t'go t'Russia, Matty. But yer Gran won't. I know one of us has to be a little bit sensible – but we're in our dotage, why ever not?

Eileen Jolyon.

Jolyon She hates anyone with a dream.

Matty *puts the egg back in the box.*

Matty Thank you for the cake.

Eileen You're welcome.

Jolyon She does. Always has.

Eileen Would you like another piece?

Matty I've had sufficient, thanks.

Eileen You're an old bugger, Jolyon. Stop it.

Jolyon (*quietly*) I'm an old bugger.

Eileen Stop asking Matty to take sides, it isn't fair.

Jolyon What d'you think? You'd go, wouldn't you?

A slight pause.

Matty I'd go, Gran. I think I would.

Jolyon There you are, love.

Matty I didn't mean I'd definitely go.

Eileen Since that television programme, Matty, we've had nothing but this.

Jolyon What's wrong with it?

Eileen If you think we can up and gallivant across the world without a thought, you've got another think coming.

Matty *looks down.*

Is that clear?

Jolyon No.

Matty *takes an egg from the box.*

Eileen He doesn't say how we can possibly afford an expensive holiday like that. We can't, and that's all there is to it. I wish we could.

Jolyon At least let's dream about it.

Matty *plays with the egg in his fingers.*

Can't we dream? Have another look at the brochure?

Eileen I'm heartily sick of being made the scapegoat.

Eileen *looks down.*

Jolyon Don't get yourself upset, love.

Eileen I am now.

Eileen *looks up.*

What was that fruit-cake like?

Matty It was delicious.

Eileen When I looked I'd only half a packet of raisins.

A slight pause.

Jolyon I wanted to show Matty the eggs. We haven't seen him for a while. We miss you when you're at school.

Matty *smiles nervously.*

Jolyon *puts the box on the ground, he stands up, and goes to* **Eileen**.

Come on, don't be silly.

Eileen I don't want you, Jolly.

Jolyon *kneels.*

Jolyon Come on, no one means anything by it, least of all me.

He takes the lace-making board and puts it on the ground.

Matty can have the eggs an' then it's a finish, isn't it? I'm only joking.

Eileen *stands up, she picks up Matty's plate, and then goes into the house.*

A pause.

Jolyon *stands up.*

I'm for the rolling-pin treatment later.

Matty *looks up.*

She's all right, don't you worry.

Matty Is she?

Jolyon Yes.

A slight pause.

Matty Did Gran know Aram?

Jolyon No, she didn't. Yer gran lived in Grange Road, which was about a mile an' a half away.

He smiles.

All that part of town is unrecognisable now. Our first home together was in Bolckow Street, near the old Albert Park. It had seventeen poplars, which were notorious for shenanagins. Your mother was born at Bolckow Street. That was razed too, eventually.

Matty *pulls the box towards himself.*

Matty May I have the eggs? You did just say?

Jolyon Yes.

Matty I'd like to do some still-life water-colours this summer. Mum's bought me an easel.

Jolyon Is this a new idea?

Matty Well, not really. I've always been fairly good. Well, it's quite new.

Jolyon Have you any you could show us?

Matty I never thought. I have some – but you mustn't laugh.

Jolyon Why?

Matty Well, it's so embarrassing – because I did some portraits of myself. Mum found them. Only I did them when I had nothing on.

A slight pause.

Jolyon That's all right. What's wrong with that?

Matty Well, at least it was a year ago. If I was excellent it probably wouldn't matter. Vanity's fine when you're talented. I don't mean they're bad or anything. Juvenile, I think. You know, doing that. (*He has gone bright pink.*) Actually, Mum thought they were rather good.

Jolyon (*smiling*) They must be then. How is your Mum?

Matty She's still laughing at me.

Jolyon Why don't you laugh back?

Matty (*smiling*) Well, I've tried.

Jolyon What happens?

Matty She laughs even more.

Jolyon I wish Eileen would laugh a little bit.

He sits on his chair.

I'm having trouble with my peeing, Matty. That's what that is all about. It's getting me down, but Eileen is beside herself with worry. I said to her: we need a plumber, love. My joke about going to Russia has nothing t'do with it.

Matty Mum told me.

Jolyon Yer gran is frightened, very understandably, I think. Embarrassed. Normally embarrassment is the other way about. For the first time in many years it's as if she seems to blame me. To be honest with you, I'm a little bit bitter about it. Very bitter. With her I mean. It started a few months ago with little splashes in my pants.

Matty Yes.

Jolyon It's me who has to leave the room. I'm the baby. I'm the one who dribbles. I think we could afford a foreign holiday if we sold the boat. I know she isn't worth very much.

Matty No.

Jolyon I wanted to ask you –

Matty What?

Jolyon If you'd help me paint her and varnish her in these next few weeks?

Matty Yes.

Jolyon It needn't take us more than a few days. We'd

have her spanking new in no time.

Matty I've been sailing at school.

Jolyon Have you? Whereabouts?

Matty Well, only on the river, tacking up and down.

Jolyon What in?

Matty An Enterprise.

Jolyon They're not dissimilar. Did you enjoy it?

Matty I enjoyed it, quite.

Jolyon You're not a sailor, are you?

Matty I escaped rugger.

Jolyon Don't you like it?

Matty Rugger? I bloody hate it.

Jolyon I meant the school, you nit.

Matty Oh, I like the school. It positively drips with well-being. I think my problem with Mum is that I'm cocooned a little. She from me, I mean.

Jolyon Why's that?

Matty I'm not unique. We have discussed it a fair bit. Most boys feel their families don't really listen to them. Or know them. I wish Mum wasn't so liberal sometimes.

Jolyon Are you wanting to be told off?

Matty I'm not saying that. Actually, I wouldn't mind occasionally.

Jolyon *smiles.*

Jolyon D'you think yer Gran an' me don't listen to you?

A slight pause.

Matty No.

Jolyon What a liar.

Matty Liar?

Jolyon Yes. Liar.

A slight pause.

Matty You leave me no option but to say 'yes' then.

Jolyon True?

Matty It might not be true. I don't know, Grandpa.

Eileen *enters from the house. She is carrying a small plate with a piece of fruit-cake on it.*

Eileen Guess who's here?

Tessa *enters. She is carrying two more, similar kitchen chairs.*

Tessa *is a tall, thin, obviously well-heeled woman of forty-six. She is wearing a summer skirt, a blouse, and expensive sandals.*

Jolyon *stands up.*

Jolyon We were just talking about you, love. Here, let me have those.

He takes the chairs from her.

Eileen I've told her what a lovely surprise it is.

Matty *stands up.*

Jolyon One for you, Matty.

Matty *takes a chair from him.* **Jolyon** *puts the other chair down.*

Tessa *sees the eggs in the box and bends over to look at them.*

Tessa Are these the Siberian eggs, Dad? They're much smaller than I imagined. Much more nondescript.

Tessa *picks up an egg.*

Matty He's given them to me.

Tessa Have you heard from the BBC at all?

Matty Careful.

Jolyon We haven't, not yet.

Tessa Perhaps they'll still have sent it on to Moscow?

Eileen He shouldn't build 'is hopes up.

Tessa It's not so far these days. I would've thought a letter had a chance.

Eileen He gets disappointed.

Jolyon Nowhere in the world is very far. I keep telling 'er that.

Eileen It's not very far on the television. It's a long way if you have to travel.

Tessa I don't think he's about to gallop off. Or are you?

Eileen I think we should trot somewhere nearer.

Jolyon We're going to see. We would like a holiday abroad. At some point.

Matty I thought I'd do some water-colours. Find a setting for them.

Tessa Are you sure, Jolly?

Jolyon Yes.

Eileen Don't let him have them if you're not sure.

Jolyon I was going to give them to him.

Tessa *puts the egg back in the box.*

Eileen *gives* **Tessa** *the plate.* **Tessa** *holds it.*

Tessa Have the eggs aged at all?

Jolyon I can't really remember, you know. I was half

surprised when there they were.

Eileen It only took him a few minutes. In the loft. I remember thinking he'd be up there all day.

Jolyon Eileen kept calling up: had I found them?

Eileen You ought to look, there might be some things you would like.

Tessa I can't think what.

Eileen Aren't there some photographs?

Jolyon Yes. Of both you, and Stephen.

Eileen You might be interested, love.

Matty Yes.

Jolyon Stephen wore your dresses, you know. I'd forgotten.

Eileen Lads won't even wear hand-me-downs these days.

Tessa Who can blame them?

Eileen Certainly not me. I don't wish what we went through on anybody.

Matty He wore Mum's dresses?

Eileen Only when he was a toddler, an' only about the house.

Tessa The street didn't know.

Eileen The street did know. Everyone did the same if you had opposite sexes. Yer just didn't let them out. One or two liked it so much, they kept it up.

Jolyon Don't exaggerate.

Eileen They did. I know of one who jumped off the transporter bridge. That was the sort of world we lived in.

Matty Was he a transvestite?

Eileen I've always had a nose for the oddities.

Jolyon You didn't tell me?

Eileen You never asked, you didn't need t'know. He'd just got used to dresses, being a boy amongst all those older girls.

Matty Was he treally a transvestite?

Eileen I was the shoulder in Bolckow Street, Matty. It was a long time ago.

A slight pause.

Jolyon Sit down. Come on.

Jolyon *sits in his chair,* **Eileen** *in hers.* **Eileen** *picks up her lace-making board.*

Tessa *begins to eat her cake.*

Tessa What're you making?

Eileen It's some lace for a paperweight.

Tessa *and* **Matty** *sit in their chairs.*

We've sold quite a few, haven't we?

Jolyon Yes. Eileen an' me got married in Bolckow Street.

A slight pause.

Yer know Eileen an' me got married because we had to. An' then the baby was stillborn. It was a lovely looking thing yer gran said. They tried not to let 'er see it, but yer know what yer gran's like. Especially then.

Tessa Dad. Honestly.

Jolyon There was another stillborn after the first. Two girls they would have been. Eileen said to me: they can't have grown dead. To this day we don't know why. I've often wondered. I like patterns, you know. I always look for the pattern in a thing.

He leans forward.

When your mum was pregnant with you, Tessa, she said: this time we don't get Mrs Colling, we get a different midwife. But in the event, you were early, so we had to. She was just round the corner in Newport Road. As I fetched 'er back I could see 'er sweating. We came in an' yer mam wouldn't have anything t'do with 'er. I said: I can't do it, Eileen. She said: you'll bloody well have to. Mrs Colling was in the kitchen, she called up the stairs: I'm going. It was pandemonium. And then yer mother called down: you'll have to do me after all, this bloody bugger is next to useless. And so she did, an' it was you. I think we knew all along it wasn't Mrs Colling, but you always look for a pattern, don't you?

Tessa Dad.

Jolyon *sits back.*

Jolyon In those days, Matty, men weren't involved. We kept out of it. I'd have liked to have seen a baby born. We saw one on the television, didn't we, Eileen? It was fascinating.

He leans forward.

D'you remember the damp in Bolckow Street?

Tessa Yes, I do.

Jolyon Yer mum used to say it was like living in the middle of a waterfall.

He sits back.

We moved here when yer mum was four and Stephen was two. It was a step up for us then. The neighbours were really stand-offish and snooty, thinking yer gran was common. She cleaned this house from top to bottom with yer mum and Stephen hanging on to her pinny.

He leans forward.

You were like a limpet, Tess. It took her three days. When she'd finished she went out into the road, stood in the middle of it, and bellowed, 'my house is cleaner than yours - there's a ten shilling note for anyone who can find even a speck of dirt in my house or on my children.' You were washed and scrubbed for the occasion, so she knew she was right. No one did come out, but yer mam had made her point.

Eileen *looks up from her lace-making, she has tears in her eyes.*

Scene Two

The backyard. A hot early August afternoon.

Three of the kitchen chairs are set apart from one another.

Matty, *wearing a sweatshirt, is standing by himself.*

Tessa *enters.*

Tessa Jolly's just died.

A pause.

Matty I'm sorry, Mum.

A pause.

Eileen *enters.*

Eileen I've put two 10p's on 'is eyes, these new pennies aren't weighty enough. It was lucky I had them in my purse.

A slight pause.

I'll wash 'im, lay 'im out. I don't want the undertaker thinking anything of us.

Tessa I'll help you.

Matty I'm sorry, Gran.

Eileen It seems funny 'im dying during the day. You expect them to die at night, don't you? Jolly never did the obvious. This baking weather got 'im down.

A slight pause.

He stole from my purse once, you know. Stole my money. You were seven, Tessa. It was three years after we'd moved here. He took five shillings from my purse an' went to Scarborough. Except I didn't know it was Scarborough when he went. He left a note on the draining-board which said: 'I've gone to find work – I'll send back what I can – Look after the bairns – Jolly.' It was our last five shillings. I'd earned that money skivvying up at Linthorpe Grange. When he got back, I said: how did you get on? He said: I looked at the sea. I said: is that all yer daft bugger? He said: yes. I said: what did you spend the five shillings on? He said: the bus fares. I said: there's men down this street walk fifteen miles to scrat f'bits of coal no larger than yer fingernail. He said: those same men beat the hell out their bairns. I said: you touch my bairns and that's it. He said: that's why I went to Scarborough. I said: it's cost me five shillings 'f'you not t'beat the bairns? He said: yes. Then there was a loud clout from next-door as Mr Troop battered their Keith. I thought: mebbe it is five shillings well spent. I said: how often are you going to need five shillings? He said: never again.

She sits down.

I came down that night and he was sitting huddled in the chair with a blanket over him. I thought: yer not so bad as to go forgetting to put my coal on my fire, because there it was burning in the grate. I said: Jolly, if you'd been able to control yourself, or put a sleeve on your doodah, we might never had wed. He said: yes. I said: we can't go on hating each other. He said: no. I said: if you ever want five shillings again you must ask.

A slight pause.

Matty Did he?

Eileen Only once, when Stephen was knocked over by that brick lorry. Stephen was the apple in his eye. He thought it wasn't fair, but then so much isn't, is it? He came and he said: I need to go, Eileen. I said: is there no more I can do, love? He said: no, you've done your best.

Matty Where did he go?

Eileen Scarborough.

Matty To look at the sea again?

Eileen Yes. When he got back, he said: I don't want Stephen's name mentioned in this house again. After five years, I thought: this is bloody daft. I said: Stephen would want us to remember him. Yer grandad said: yes, I was wrong. And that was it.

A slight pause.

Matty Is that why he bought the sailing dinghy?

Eileen He bought the boat to be on the sea. He could go anywhere in that boat. In his head, Matty, in his dreams.

Tessa *picks up a chair, she sits down beside* **Eileen**.

Tessa I think you should come and stay with us for a few days.

Eileen I won't, pet. The only way to get used to an empty house is to live in it.

A slight pause.

Matty I'll go, and come back, Mum.

Tessa All right.

Matty *goes into the house.*

Eileen I'm glad it's this way round. He could do scrambled egg, and that was it. D'you think I stopped him dreaming, Tess?

Tessa Of course not.

Eileen I did, you know.

A slight pause.

Tessa Mum, I think your own doctor should write a death certificate. I'm not certain I can. Don't you worry about it, I'll ring him.

Eileen Will you?

Tessa Yes.

Eileen Don't listen to 'im if 'e goes on about yer dad. It'll be stuff and nonsense.

Tessa Dad came to me about his incontinence. It's very, very common, there's nothing to be ashamed of.

Eileen I didn't know that?

Tessa He didn't want you worried.

Eileen I was worried.

Tessa I know you were.

Eileen Then why didn't you tell me?

Tessa He asked me not to.

Eileen Did he ring you?

Tessa Yes. He came to the hospital. We looked at him properly.

Eileen I didn't know any of this, Tess.

A slight pause.

Tessa I asked him to tell you, but he wouldn't.

Eileen Why?

Tessa I don't know, Mum.

Eileen He was getting his own back, wasn't he?

Tessa That's very silly.

Eileen Is it?

Tessa You must know it is.

Eileen I don't.

A slight pause.

Jolly was very bitter, you know. He thought life had let him down.

Tessa Did he?

Eileen He was very bitter. I'd be a fool if I didn't know that I was his life.

Tessa I think you're twisting things, Mum.

Eileen Twisting what?

Tessa Twisting your memories.

A slight pause.

When I was seven, Jolly was working. You've nothing to feel guilty about.

Eileen He wanted to study, you know. He always did. We couldn't afford it. All my life that's what I've said. When you went off to university, he shone like the sun. He said: I wanted Stephen to be the doctor, but now it's our Tess.

A slight pause.

I just worried you'd fall into bad company.

Tessa I didn't, did I?

Eileen No, you've made your life very good. He was proud of you.

A slight pause.

He could always meet you, Tess. D'you know what I mean?

Tessa Not really, I don't.

Eileen In intelligence, up here.

Eileen *taps her head.*

I've wanted to say this for a long time. Not say, so much as admit. For most of my life I've been a very jealous woman.

Tessa Mum –

Eileen If yer dad had been on his own – this is true, Tess – you'd have come home much more often. I've seen yer dad broken because you didn't come home.

Tessa *looks down, and then she looks back up.*

Tessa Why don't we wait before we say these things?

Eileen I want you to understand that I do know what I'm like.

Tessa Mum –

Eileen Jolly used to say that you make time for the things you really want to do. You didn't come home because of me. That is the truth, isn't it?

Tessa I've had my career. And Matty. I've wanted him to grow up responsibly and strong.

Eileen Yes.

Tessa It isn't you. Now isn't the time. Not for recrimination.

Eileen I'm worried there never will be a time. Yer dad used to say: our Tess has outgrown us, Eileen. I used to say: she's flown the nest, pet.

A slight pause.

If I was him sitting here you'd be telling him the truth, wouldn't you? I've always kept the truth away.

A slight pause.

He was such a dreamer. It was me who made the ends meet. I was busy running the family.

A slight pause.

I used to think: we'll not have a family if I let him dream – we'll be out on the streets – we'll be begging. Isn't that stupid? I'm sorry, Tess.

Tessa It isn't stupid, Mum.

Eileen It is, you know.

A slight pause.

I suppose the one thing I've learnt – is that somehow you do get by. That must be true, because we did.

Tessa Yes.

Eileen I am sorry.

Tessa You've nothing to be sorry for.

Eileen I have, you know.

A slight pause.

Tessa It's Dr Cottie, isn't it, Mum?

Eileen Mmm?

Tessa Your doctor. Dr Cottie?

Eileen Yes, it is.

Scene Three

Later that day.

At the top of a sloping, shingle beach is a wooden sign saying: Tees Sailing Club. Below the sign is a lifebelt hanging onto a hook on the same pole. On the shingle is a G.P.14 sailing dinghy. It is standing on its metal launching trolley.

Evening. It is very still. There are long shadows from the sun.

Matty *is standing looking at the sea. He has the box under his arm, and white paint on his hands.*

Jolyon *is beside the boat. He is painting the hull with a brush and a pot of white paint. He has paint on his hands. He is wearing a white woodworking apron which gives him a slightly ghostly appearance.*

A slight pause.

Matty Can I ask you something, Grandpa?

Jolyon *paints.*

Jolyon It depends what it is.

Matty Would you still marry Eileen?

Jolyon *paints.*

Jolyon That's a question and a half, isn't it?

Jolyon *paints.*

Matty *sits down. He takes an egg from the box and plays with it between his fingers.*

Matty But you learnt to love her, didn't you?

Jolyon I think so. Yes.

Jolyon *paints.*

Matty That's all I wanted to know really.

Jolyon *paints.*

Matty *runs the egg between his fingers.*

Jolyon *puts the brush on top of the paint pot.*

Jolyon I must go. Nature calls again.

Jolyon *goes.*

Matty *puts the egg back into the box. He stands up, goes to the boat, and puts the box on the bow. He picks up the paint brush and continues to paint.*

A pause.

Tessa *enters.*

Matty You were bloody mad.

Tessa Who was mad?

Matty *looks up.*

Matty Where did you come from?

Tessa I've been searching high and low for you.

Matty I've been here, doing this.

Tessa *joins him.*

I was thinking about Grandpa, that was all.

Tessa Why was he mad?

Matty Look in the dinghy.

Tessa *looks in the boat.*

Matty *puts the brush on top of the paint pot. He takes a cardboard box from the boat. It is full of tinned and packet foods. He puts the box on the shingle, kneels, and takes from it tins of soup, meat, vegetables, and fruit. Eventually he upends the box and the rest of the tins and packets tumble out.*

He was stocking up. He was planning to sail to Russia.

Tessa Matty, why didn't you tell me?

Matty He made me promise not to.

*He stands up and takes another cardboard box from the boat.
He puts it down and kneels. He takes pots and pans, a tin-
opener, and a portable gas-ring from it.*

I think towards the end he was going senile. Was he,
Mum?

Tessa Where was he getting all this?

Matty He was buying it. It's all new.

Tessa *kneels.*

Tessa He must've known what he was doing, didn't he?
It was probably a little joke with himself.

Matty Some joke.

Tessa Yes, I agree.

Matty Actually, I don't think it was. He was very serious
about going to Russia.

He stands.

I've been trying to slow us down. I've been painting as
badly as I could.

He takes two plastic water-carriers from the boat.

Then something else would appear.

Tessa It's certainly perverse.

Matty *kneels.*

Matty I think he was going.

Tessa No, he wasn't.

Matty He was.

Tessa No. He was getting his own back. In his own quiet
way he was being a little bit spiteful.

Matty Spiteful?

Tessa Yes.

Matty To who?

Tessa To your grandmother, I think. To Eileen, probably.

Matty But I don't think she knows, Mum.

Tessa No. I don't expect she does.

Matty How can it be spiteful then?

A slight pause.

Tessa It was the way he learnt to cope with her. To wander off on his own periodically and do his own thing.

Matty Be perverse, you mean?

Tessa It certainly looks like it, doesn't it?

Matty Yes. Why?

A slight pause.

Tessa Oh, I suspect he felt bossed about. Eileen can be bossy, can't she?

Matty Sometimes.

Tessa I suspect he occasionally felt stifled by her. And I don't blame him.

A slight pause.

Matty What d'you mean by stifled.

A slight pause.

Tessa Oh, I think he wanted more from the world than just Eileen.

A slight pause.

Matty You feel like grandpa, don't you? About gran, I mean.

A slight pause.

I asked him if he'd still marry her?

Tessa What was his reply?

Matty He said he thought so. Then nature called. We're a funny family.

Tessa I asked him once. A long time ago.

Matty What did he say?

Tessa He said: no.

A slight pause.

It was a weekend he came on his own to visit me at university.

Matty In London?

Tessa Yes. Eileen was being particularly savage to him. He sat on my bed and cried.

Matty What about?

Tessa It was actually about getting a television. Jolly would always spend money, if they had it. It seems strange now when you think how their life together revolved around the television.

Matty Yes.

Tessa What was on it. What programmes they saw. They viewed the world from the television.

A slight pause.

Matty Is that what made Jolly bitter, Mum?

Tessa What?

Matty I don't know really – seeing places like Russia – and not being able to go?

Tessa I think it did make him bitter, yes.

Matty *stands up.*

Matty Gran said he could go anywhere in this boat. He couldn't though, could he?

Tessa No.

Matty He knew he couldn't, didn't he?

Tessa Yes.

Matty He was just a poor old fucker who wanted to enjoy himself.

Tessa Matty.

Matty He was though, wasn't he?

A slight pause.

Tessa I think so, darling.

A slight pause.

We must be very, very careful with my mum during the next few weeks.

Matty Is she going to come and stay?

Tessa No, she won't.

Matty Why?

Tessa I suspect she's probably better off in her own home.

Matty You don't like her very much, do you, Mum?

A slight pause.

Tessa Matty, I can't face much more of this. I came to find you because I thought you'd be a comfort.

A slight pause.

Matty *goes to his mother, he touches her on the arm.*

Matty Would you like a drink? Mmm? I can go to the bar.

Tessa Have you some money?

Matty I've got some.

Matty *goes.*

A pause.

Tessa *stands up.*

Matty *returns.*

They won't serve me. It's that horrible fat barman on.

Tessa Have you even looked at any schoolwork this summer?

Matty *shrugs.*

Matty I've been too busy.

Tessa I thought not. What happened to that reading list you had, and the cheque I gave you?

Matty I put it in my deposit account.

Tessa It won't buy a book there, will it?

Matty It's getting the interest.

Tessa That's not the point.

Matty I will, Mum, don't worry.

Tessa Yes, I've heard that before, too.

Matty Don't get at me, please. I'm very good when I want to be.

Tessa *smiles.*

Tessa Yes, you are really.

Matty Actually, Mum, it's possible to buy them half price, from pupils who've just left.

Tessa Doesn't that mean you wouldn't have them until the beginning of term?

Matty Well, not quite. Actually, they hold the sale at the end of term. Last term, I mean.

Tessa So you've bought them already? You are a cheat, Matty.

Matty I only bought one or two. Not all of them.

Tessa Where are they?

Matty I left them at school.

Tessa Had you no intention of doing any work?

Matty I'm going to read the ones I have to buy here. I thought I'd better tell you, that was all.

Tessa Yes. I'm not sure I approve.

Matty It seemed sensible, don't you think?

Tessa I expect so.

Matty They're only for reading round the subject. It's just better to have your own.

Tessa You don't need to convince me.

Matty Thanks, Mum.

Tessa *smiles.*

I'm sorry about just now – you know – being unfeeling and things.

Tessa I was very fond of him.

Matty I thought I might try and write a pamphlet about Grandpa. Like those thirties pamphlets of his.

Tessa A pamphlet?

Matty It wouldn't be very good. I don't mean to be big-headed.

Tessa *smiles.*

A history, sort of thing – about how the eggs might have

come from Russia. Don't you think it's a good idea?

Tessa It's very good.

Matty Don't patronise me, Mum.

Tessa I wasn't. It is a good idea.

Matty I had a look in the library and I think the most likely way was with a trade delegation – the mysterious Russian must have been an entrepreneur. I thought I'd start with that.

Tessa *smiles.*

Tessa I'm sorry, darling, I'm just very tired. I've had a difficult afternoon with Eileen.

Matty Is she all right?

Tessa Not really. I don't know what to do. I wonder if we shouldn't go now, and insist she comes back with us?

Matty *shrugs.*

Matty If she doesn't want to come –

Tessa She keeps going on about it being an empty house.

A slight pause.

Matty I don't know, I'm not an expert. Have they taken him?

Tessa Yes, the undertaker's been.

Matty So his body's not there?

Tessa No. We did all that very well.

Matty Did you really have to wash him?

Tessa Yes.

Matty I don't know how you could. (*He has pulled a face.*)

Tessa All the neighbours know.

Matty *kneels. He begins to put the tins and pans back into their boxes.*

I think what we'll do is call in, Matty. If you don't mind?

Matty No.

Tessa Suggest she comes for the evening, and then I'll run her home if she doesn't want to stay.

Matty Yes.

Tessa I suspect if we get her there, she will.

Matty I think that's best, too.

Tessa Do you?

Matty I've just said so, Mum.

Tessa We'd better take all this with us. No, we hadn't, we'd better leave it in the boat.

Tessa *helps* **Matty.**

Matty *lifts the boxes and the water-carriers into the boat.*

Matty It probably would've sunk anyway – all this stuff in it.

Tessa Where did he say he was sailing to?

Matty Siberia.

Tessa It's not on the sea.

Matty I know.

Tessa And you took him seriously?

Matty Well, I didn't, not quite. If you're thinking of sailing to Siberia it doesn't really matter whether it's on the sea or not, does it?

Tessa *smiles.*

Tessa Poor you.

Matty *takes the box from the bow of the boat and gives it to* **Tessa** *to hold. He puts the lid on the pot of paint.*

I haven't seen you using the easel?

Matty *puts the paint pot into the boat. He finds a jar of turpentine, and puts the brush in that.*

Matty I thought I might sell it.

Tessa Have you used it at all, Matty?

Matty *takes a green canvas cover from inside the boat. He begins to fit it, first at the stern, and then at the bow.*

Matty Well, not really, Mum. I haven't had much time.

Tessa It isn't good enough, you know.

Matty Well, I thought if I sold it – it is a good idea, don't you think?

Tessa No, I don't.

A slight pause.

Matty I have other things I need much more.

Tessa It was a very expensive easel and you're absolutely not going to sell it. Have I made myself plain?

A slight pause.

Matty I think we should at least consider it.

Tessa Matty.

Matty What?

Tessa Shut up.

A slight pause.

Matty Well, I thought if we sold it we could buy a printer for the computer. I'm mainly thinking of you – you know how you're always grumbling.

Tessa Matty.

Matty What?

Tessa I have said 'no'.

Matty Oh, don't be silly. You're always saying we need a printer.

Tessa I have never said that.

Matty You have, Mum.

Tessa Matty.

Matty What?

Tessa One more word and I'll clout you. Is that clear?

Matty *stops, he looks up at her.*

Matty It isn't very fair. I'm only doing my best, you know.

Tessa I know you do your best.

Matty Well then –

Tessa No.

Matty Oh, Mum.

Tessa This time it's no, darling. You're getting away with far too much.

Matty Me?

Tessa Matty, if you don't shut up I'll take back the money you made on those school books.

Matty *continues to fit the canvas cover.*

Matty What's come over you?

Tessa Nothing.

Matty Is it my fault?

A slight pause.

Is it Jolly?

Tessa No, darling, it's you. You're becoming a manipulator, and I'm not having it.

Matty *stops, he looks up.*

Matty You can do this on your own then. I'm going.

Matty *goes.*

A slight pause.

Tessa *walks to the boat. She continues to fit the canvas cover.*

Scene Four

Tees Sailing Club. A hot late August afternoon.

The G.P.14 sailing dinghy is painted and varnished. Its cover is off. Nearby, on a thin pole pushed into the shingle, is a cardboard sign saying: For sale.

Matty, *wearing a t-shirt, is standing one side of the dinghy.*

Eileen, *wearing a cotton dress, is standing the other. Nearby is a picnic basket.*

Matty We did a good job, don't you think?

Eileen Yes, she looks lovely.

Matty We had her stripped right down. Well, grandpa did most of it.

Eileen Jolly built her himself.

Matty I know. From a kit.

Eileen That's right. One summer. In our backyard. Come the end of August he had to knock part of a wall down to get her out. It was a terrible palaver. The whole road came out, it was such a sight. Then half of them wanted a go. A sail. So Jolly took them out, one by one. Most of them faded away when they realised it meant gettin' yer bum all wet.

She smiles.

When we were racing, Matty, he'd always want to win, so you got hollered at as well. I said to him once: why can't we come second, Jolly? Second wasn't in his nature.

Matty Did he win?

Eileen Most often he did. It was the sheer joy 'e got from it. He never settled, you know, when he got too old to sail. He missed it like anything. I know he did. Jolly wasn't a spectator.

Matty Is she worth any less because she was built from a kit?

Eileen I don't see why.

Matty You must make sure you get more than they offer.

Eileen Isn't a thing worth what someone will pay for it?

Matty I'm just warning you.

Eileen I don't need warning, thank you.

Matty I'd ask for at least a hundred pounds more.

Eileen Yes, well –

Matty It's the way business is done.

Eileen Is it? In that case I might leave it up to you. He'll probably take one look at you and think: here's a silly boy, I can get it a hundred pounds cheaper.

Matty That isn't very fair.

Eileen Don't you answer me back either.

Matty I wasn't. I was thinking of you.

Eileen I will get what is right. You're far too quick to jump on to money.

Matty (*quietly, turning away*) Yes, Gran. Three bags full, Gran.

Eileen (*going to him*) Now, I didn't mean to spoil our day. So let's forget it, shall we?

Tessa *enters wearing a summer dress. She is carrying three drinks: a light ale, a vodka and orange, and a half pint of lager.*

Tessa I've told them that if anyone asks, we're down here.

Matty *takes the lager from her.*

Matty Thanks, Mum.

Eileen *takes the light ale.*

Eileen It feels like a holiday to be having a drink. Thank you. I will get us one later.

Pavel *enters.*

Pavel *is a tall, slightly stocky man of fifty-nine, whose hair is receding. He is wearing a dark suit, a tie, and a white shirt.*

Pavel *stops.*

Pavel Mrs Davis?

Tessa This is Mrs Davis.

Pavel *steps forward.*

Pavel Dear lady, my name is Professor Pavel Kabalevsky, I am the director of the Oka nature reserve.

A slight pause.

I am so sorry if I have interrupted you.

A slight pause.

Tessa No, it's all right.

Pavel (*to* **Tessa**) I have called at this lady's house, but no, she is not there, you understand me?

Tessa Yes.

Pavel (*to* **Eileen**) A neighbour of yours, I think, she says you are here, so here I come following the road. She says sometimes you are at home, and sometimes with your daughter. My time here is very short, I have only one day, you understand me?

Eileen Yes.

Pavel It is urgent for me. Then I must go to Baraboo, Wisconsin, America. But I am so excited by this letter, dear lady, it is the greatest excitement.

Eileen Yes.

Pavel *takes the letter from the inside pocket of his jacket.*

Pavel This letter, you know, it is waiting for me at the BBC in Bristol. I go to Bristol before going to Baraboo, Wisconsin, America. I talk with the BBC, maybe, about making another film. But I do not know. I do not think so now. It cost so much money, you understand me?

Eileen I understand.

Pavel Good. So I am here and I would like it very much to meet your husband.

Eileen Yes.

A slight pause.

Pavel My time here is very short. Only one day.

Tessa I'm Mrs Davis's daughter.

Pavel It is a pleasure to meet you all.

Matty I'm Matthew.

Pavel How do you all do.

Pavel *shakes hands with them.*

Now I would like it very much to meet Mr Davis.

Tessa Mr Davis died a fortnight ago.

A slight pause.

Pavel He is not here?

He turns to **Eileen**.

I am so sorry. For you, dear lady, I am so very sorry.

Eileen He passed away very suddenly, didn't he?

Tessa Yes.

Matty After he'd written to you. Mr Davis wanted to go to Russia.

A slight pause.

Pavel I was intrigued by his letter, you understand me? The White Siberian Crane it is nearly all my life for over ten years. I criss-cross the world in my endeavour to return this bird to his natural place. We are on the very brink of success. This letter, somehow, it make me think about what has gone before, you understand me? This is why I come. I think this man – Mr Davis – he has a part of my history, somehow. You understand?

Eileen Yes.

Pavel I am not the relation he thinks. I do not know these other people he writes to me about. It is not for that reason I come, you understand?

Eileen Yes.

Pavel But I like to meet the man who has these eggs. I want to ask him if he loves the birds as I do. I think so from his letter. That I like very much. My desire is a very simple one.

Eileen Yes.

A slight pause.

Pavel But I have interrupted you, dear people.

Tessa No. Would you like a drink?

Pavel I would like very much a pint of your English bitter, please. Thank you.

Tessa *puts her glass on the bow of the boat.*

Your English pubs fascinate me.

Tessa *smiles and goes.*

When I am with the BBC we go into pubs all the time for discussions.

Eileen I remember you from the television.

Pavel Sometimes I am so nervous I get wrong what I have to say, and they shout 'cut', and we have to start again.

Matty Are you making another programme?

Pavel I have tried to say I do not think so. I am very disappointed by this. I look for a way of telling my story, you understand. These birds are very important.

Eileen We enjoyed it.

Pavel Thank you. It is shown in the Soviet Union, too. We, too, have our wildlife programmes for people to be educated about ecology. This is most important.

Matty How did they film it?

Pavel They come to my home. I live in the little village of Brukin Bor, which is on the Pra river. This is the centre of the Oka nature reserve. At first they do the background. They ask the local children to be jolly in the river for them. This they shoot. And the women drawing water from the well, too. We always hear a cry of 'hair in the gate'. So, like 'cut', everyone has to do it again. By now the children are blue. The Pra river is very cold in April. It made me laugh, you know, because they are blue and shivering, and getting them to take a hot bath is sometimes difficult. Mothers, I think, must make a camera, and say 'turn over' when it is bath-time. But this you saw on the film, dear lady?

Eileen Yes.

Pavel We are fascinated to have this camera in our lives.

Eileen Television's a wonderful thing, isn't it?

Pavel I think this is so.

Matty How long were they there?

Pavel For three weeks. Once the women have drawn the water from the well, and the cart has come along the lane, and the man has ridden his motorbike over the humps, and the boy has tethered his grandfather's cow, and the girl has chased her chickens – then we go into the Oka reserve to film the wildlife. The wildlife there is very special for me. I dream of the day I see the White Siberian Crane.

Tessa *enters with a pint of bitter.* **Pavel** *puts the letter back in his pocket and takes his drink.*

I must thank you, dear lady. I must thank you all for being so kind already.

He drinks some beer.

This, it is delicious.

Matty Why are you going to America?

Pavel It is here, now, in America, that there is a flock of Siberian Cranes. Ten years ago we have taken four eggs from the north of Siberia. In Baraboo, Wisconsin, they have hatched these rare eggs, and raised the chicks by hand. These chicks are now mature, and they are laying eggs of their own. I must go to prepare. This spring they will take these eggs. I, myself, will go once more to America. In an incubator I will carry the eggs back to the Oka reserve. There, we will go deep into the forests, and we will put them on to the nest of the Grey Crane. He is very common, not so special. You understand the cuckoo, dear people?

Matty Yes.

Pavel We hope the Grey Crane will be a cuckoo for the Siberian Crane eggs. He will hatch, and raise the chicks as his own. In this way, we save this bird from extinction. If we are successful he will go on growing in the wild. I am very optimistic now.

Pavel *smiles. He drinks some beer.*

Tessa When do you go back to the Soviet Union?

Pavel I have one week only in America. I miss my family very much. Unfortunately it is not possible for them to accompany me, you understand? My son he is only fourteen. He has his school and must do well at that.

He smiles.

Also, my English, it is taught to me by my wife. My wife, she is from England many years ago. This makes it doubly difficult for me to travel. I have many difficulties at first. They want to know everything. It took me eight years. I am very privileged.

He smiles.

My wife, she is brought up in Royal Tunbridge Wells. I go there, too, for one day only. I like to see the streets she played in. I say to her: I know what Tunbridge Wells is like now. And she laughs, you know.

Eileen Would you like to share our picnic?

Pavel I know about English picnicking. I would like that very much.

Matty *puts his lager on the bow of the boat. He takes the green canvas cover from inside and begins to spread it on the shingle.*

Tessa *helps him.*

Is this your boat?

Eileen Yes.

Pavel Where I live we have boats, too. I live on the flood plain of the Oka river. In spring the forests are deep in water. When the snow melts, you understand me?

Eileen Yes.

Pavel I would like it very much to see these eggs if this is possible?

Eileen Matty has them.

Pavel May I ask if he is your grandchild?

Eileen Yes, he is.

Pavel He reminds me of my own boy a little. Always helpful, I think?

Eileen (*smiling*) Yes.

Pavel Good boys.

Eileen Matty, what happened to the eggs?

Matty They're at home unfortunately.

Pavel Such a pity. Another time, perhaps?

Eileen Yes.

Pavel He works hard at school, I hope?

Eileen I think so. Don't you?

Matty Sometimes.

Pavel Ah, but, sometimes is not enough.

Eileen He won't be bossed about.

Pavel That is just like my son. Independent people.

The canvas cover is spread across the shingle.

Eileen *picks up the picnic basket. They sit down around it.*

Eileen *begins to unwrap the packages of tinfoil, and spread the picnic. There are sandwiches, cakes and pieces of fruit.*

Dear people, this is the nicest day I have spent in England.

Tessa When do you leave for America?

Pavel I must go tomorrow morning.

Matty He can stay with us, can't he?

Tessa Would you like to stay with us this evening?

Pavel I have checked into a hotel. But I will cancel it. Thank you very much.

Eileen *gives them all a paper serviette.*

Eileen I didn't bother with plates. There's egg and tomato, cheese, and some chicken.

She takes a bag from the basket.

And one or two extra tomatoes here. You'll have to all dive in and help yourselves.

Pavel Mr Davis, he was an ornithologist?

A slight pause.

Tessa Mum, was dad an ornithologist?

Eileen No, he just happened to have the eggs. It was seeing you on the television that reminded him.

Pavel *smiles.*

Pavel Was it his hobby?

Eileen It wasn't even as much as that.

Pavel But he was interested a little?

Eileen Yes.

Pavel I wonder if maybe he is an ornithologist, you know. It is his friend Aram he is interested in? I understand now.

Eileen There was nothing special about Jolly.

Pavel Except, of course, to you, dear lady.

Eileen I think if you don't mind I'm going to go for a little walk.

She stands up.

I won't be very long. Help yourselves, won't you?

Tessa *stands.*

Tessa I'll come with you, Mum.

Pavel *stands.*

Eileen I'd rather go on my own, Tess.

Tessa Are you sure?

Eileen Yes. Dig in and I won't be long.

Eileen *goes.*

Pavel It is very frightening when we lose someone so close to us. I must thank you all for your hospitality, but I must go, too. I do not like to be the cause of this lady being frightened.

Tessa No. Stay.

Matty It's me, Mum. I upset her earlier.

Tessa Matty. Honestly.

Matty I didn't mean to. I'm sick of watching my p's and q's.

Pavel If I go to my hotel, dear people, perhaps I may meet you all this evening?

Tessa Stay. Please.

Matty Shall I go after her?

Tessa No.

Pavel I am worried about this lady.

Tessa There's nothing to worry about.

Pavel I am still worried.

Matty She didn't expect you, did she, Mum?

Tessa No.

Pavel I do some things and I surprise myself sometimes.

Pavel *sits down.*

Tessa I'll just go and catch her up.

Tessa *goes after* **Eileen.**

Pavel You know, I think when we are older, the world it begins to go a little faster than us.

Matty Yes.

A slight pause.

Pavel You know, now that I begin to travel and see the world, I realise so much more.

Matty Do you?

Pavel Of course. I begin to realise just how fast the world is. We are so easily left behind.

A slight pause.

If I am a shock for her – but you must tell me if this is
true about your grandmother?

Tessa *enters.*

Tessa She's very upset. She just runs away.

Tessa *sits.*

Pavel If it is me, please tell me?

Tessa It is, yes.

Pavel I am so very sorry.

Tessa My father would've loved to have visited your
country. That's all it is.

Pavel It is because I am here?

Tessa She feels guilty.

A slight pause.

Pavel I think I must go.

Tessa No. Stay.

Pavel. If I upset her?

Tessa It doesn't matter.

Matty It does her good.

Tessa That's a horrible thing to say.

Matty You've said it.

A slight pause.

Tessa I'm sorry to involve you in our squabbles.

Eileen *enters.*

Matty Are you all right, Gran?

Eileen I will be in a minute. You haven't even started.
Aren't you hungry, Mr Kabalevsky?

Pavel *stands.*

Pavel You must forgive me, dear lady.

Eileen I'm the one making a fool of myself.

She joins them.

It's very good of you to come and visit us.

Pavel I was worried, you know.

Eileen You don't have to worry about me.

Eileen *sits.*

You've come a long way, haven't you?

Pavel It is not so very far from Bristol.

Pavel *sits.*

Eileen I was meaning from Russia, Mr Kabalevsky.

Pavel The Soviet Union is a vast country, if you understand me? So many different people, so many distances.

Eileen Do we seem small here?

Pavel In my country it is a privilege to travel. You are very lucky.

Eileen I bet we must seem small really.

Pavel *smiles.*

Pavel A little. You know, it is so easy to travel around England. Even I manage this easily.

Eileen That's more than me, Mr Kabalevsky.

Pavel You do not travel so much?

Eileen No. We would've liked to. It came too late for us.

Pavel I understand. It is much the same. Do you think it is the young people who will have these things?

Eileen I do. An' good on them for it. I hope they learn something from it.

Pavel I think it is the young people, too.

A slight pause.

Eileen I didn't make this for it to go all dry.

They begin to eat the large picnic.

What d'you think about responsibility, Mr Kabalevsky?

Pavel I beg your pardon, dear lady?

Eileen It's crossed my mind that the more people have, the less responsible they are.

Pavel *thinks.*

Pavel Yes, responsibility to one's country is most important. We must all work together for the same ideals.

Matty What d'you like best about England?

Pavel I have tried to say I think it is your freedom to travel. My son, he is fourteen. I hope he will travel, too, one day very soon. I would like him to be like you, always helpful to his family.

Eileen *smiles.*

Eileen Matty's been abroad, haven't you?

Matty I've been to Greece and Portugal. And America. I went there with Mum when my father emigrated.

Pavel My son, Nikolai, would love to talk with you. He is very fond of people.

Pavel *smiles.*

Why do you only sometimes work hard at school?

A slight pause.

Matty Well, I was joking mainly.

Tessa He doesn't like to be thought of as a swot.

Pavel A swot? Does this mean you are being modest to me?

Matty Well, not really. A little, perhaps.

Pavel But I like to see modesty in young people. It is best for them.

Matty I try to be.

Pavel You like your school very much?

Matty Yes.

Pavel It is near here? But you are on your summer holiday.

Matty I attend St Peter's School in York.

Tessa He boards at a public school.

Pavel Ah. You are very privileged?

Matty Yes.

Eileen Matty's very lucky.

Pavel I understand.

A slight pause.

Dear lady, when you talk about responsibility, are you talking about the responsibility of knowing how lucky you are?

Eileen Yes, I am.

Pavel Ah. I understand you now.

Pavel *smiles.*

You know, I think the world it will belong to you young people. You must be very wise with it. I would like you very much to meet my son.

Matty *puts down his sandwich.*

Matty Mum.

Tessa Are you inviting him, Mr Kabalevsky?

Pavel I am, yes. I think we must see if this is possible.

Eileen Would you like to go, Matty?

Matty Me? You must be joking. Of course I would.

Pavel You would enjoy seeing the White Siberian Crane?

Matty Yes, not half.

Pavel Good. I will speak with some people I know.

Matty I'd love it.

Eileen What does he have t'do?

Pavel Nothing for the moment. Please, you must leave this with me. Very often I am quite lucky. But I will have to fight for it. I am a fighter, you know. All my life I have been a fighter.

Pavel, **Eileen** *and* **Tessa** *are looking at* **Matty**.

Scene Five

Later. Early evening.

A vast lawn. A single apple tree which is laden with apples. A grass rake is leaning against the tree.

A bright sun.

Eileen *is standing by herself.*

Tessa *enters. She is smoking a cigarette.*

Eileen I'm coming.

Tessa There's no hurry, I've only just put the potatoes on.

Tessa *joins* **Eileen**.

Eileen I'd like to tell you something, Tess.

Tessa What?

Eileen Watt invented steam.

Tessa I walked into that, didn't I? Mum, what d'you want to tell me? Is it important or not?

Eileen I was looking at the garden, thinking about Matty.

Tessa I know he isn't perfect, Mum, but he's all I have. Yes?

Eileen I know that, pet. We're so much at cross-purposes you and me.

Tessa We're at cross-purposes, Mum, because you will interfere. Until you learn to leave well alone we will be.

A slight pause.

Eileen That's put me in my place.

Tessa Stop being bloody manipulative. You're as bad as Matty.

Eileen I know.

Tessa Mum, if you know, why the hell do you carry on? At least he has sixteen as an excuse.

A slight pause.

Eileen All my life I feel I've been in the middle of battles.

A slight pause.

Battles for this, battles f'that. Battles to keep our heads above water. I'm so jealous of him, Tess. That's what I wanted to tell you.

She is really upset. **Tessa** *hugs her.*

Tessa Oh, Mum.

Eileen It's easier to think the right thoughts than it is to do the right things.

She is crying.

Matty *enters.*

Matty Mum, Mr Kabalevsky would – like – to – see.

Tessa I'll come and find you later, darling.

Matty Yes.

Matty *goes.*

Eileen He has the world at his feet. I just hope he succeeds, because I haven't. All my life I've been battling. Battling for you. Battling for Jolly. Battling for what is right. An' all I feel is a failure. Because if you look at the world all you see is greed. I'm very jealous of greedy people. I wish I was.

Tessa Mum –

Eileen No, it's true, Tess. I don't mean you and Matty because you're family. I really don't. You'll have to believe me.

Tessa I do.

Eileen I've always loved you all, you know.

Tessa I know.

Eileen I've always wanted the best for you all. You've had the best, Tess. And we struggled for it I can tell you.

Tessa I know, Mum. Don't be upset.

Eileen I can't help it. I'm like a coil at the moment.

Tessa Listen, if you're worried about Matty being greedy and selfish – don't. He's my responsibility, isn't he?

Eileen He seems to get everything he wants, Tess. It isn't right.

Tessa Mum, he doesn't actually.

Eileen Doesn't he?

Tessa No. He's growing up. He's got to be allowed to grow up.

Eileen I think that's what I mean, love. What's he going to be like when he's older?

Tessa Matty's very sensitive, Mum. He isn't stupid. In any case he's my responsibility. Not yours.

Eileen I can't help feeling partly responsible.

Tessa You mustn't.

Eileen No.

A slight pause.

I expect I've got everything jumbled up.

Eileen *breaks the hug.* **Tessa** *takes her hand.*

Tessa You haven't. You're doing what you think is proper. I'm very grateful.

Eileen Oh, I don't know, love. I ought to know better at my age.

Tessa Mum, it's time you enjoyed yourself. My problems, Matty's problems, they're not of your making. Are they?

Eileen No. Why do I feel so guilty then?

Tessa You mustn't carry us on your shoulders.

Eileen No.

A slight pause.

I used to think living was so simple. It isn't, is it? Mind

you, I think it used to be simpler. I don't envy Matty in a way.

A slight pause.

I think you're right – I must just try an' enjoy myself a bit more.

Tessa You must.

Eileen You won't tell him what I've said, will you?

Tessa Of course I won't.

Eileen It's all right f'me to know what a stupid woman I am – I don't want him to know it as well.

Tessa He doesn't. You're not stupid.

Eileen Oh, I am.

Tessa Mum, don't knock yourself so much.

Eileen I can't help it. It's the way I was brought up. I think what I'm jealous of is Matty's confidence.

Eileen *has tears in her eyes.* **Tessa** *hugs her.*

Tessa Come on, let's have no more.

A slight pause.

You were very confident with me when I was a child. I remember.

Eileen If I was it was all show. I didn't feel it. An' Stephen being killed like that. Why wasn't I watching him?

Tessa You couldn't be everywhere, Mum. It wasn't your fault. You've done enough for other people. These things are in the past. Think about yourself for a change.

Eileen I'm going to wear myself out, Tess.

Tessa I know you are. You mustn't. You're very

important. There's only so much one person can do.

A slight pause.

Mum, I can't treat every patient in the hospital, can I? Can I, Mum?

Eileen No, you can't love.

Tessa You're asking Herculean things of yourself. It isn't fair. You must learn to let events ride sometimes.

Eileen What gets to me is being jealous. I don't understand it.

Tessa You're not jealous, Mum. You're just worrying. You're worrying far too much. There's nothing to worry about.

Eileen No.

Eileen *breaks the hug.*

A lot of this comes from Jolly. I miss him like a massive space was gone.

Tessa I know. We all do. But he wouldn't want you to go around saying you were jealous, and all those things, would he?

Eileen I think I am a bit jealous, pet.

Tessa Well, whatever you are, it doesn't matter. What matters is the future.

Eileen Yes.

Tessa Think of something you've always wanted to do. And try and do that. And don't worry about it.

Eileen Yes.

Tessa Is there something you wished you'd done, and never have?

Eileen There must be a million things.

Tessa Don't worry about money.

Eileen There is one thing, pet.

Tessa What?

Eileen He invented steam. I'm very jealous of Matty going to Russia.

Act Two

Scene One

The small garden adjoining a wooden house at the village of Brukin Bor in the Soviet Union. A mild afternoon the following late April.

The garden has a very low (perhaps no more than six-inches high) wooden fence around it with an opening for people to come in and out. It is painted blue but the harsh winter has cracked and taken much of the life from it. Along one side of the fence is a large, neatly stacked pile of cut logs. In one or two places a slushy snow is still on the muddy ground. Everywhere is damp and drab as spring slowly thaws the earth, and nothing has much colour.

Margaret *is sitting in the garden on a wooden chair. She has a workbasket beside her and she is darning a sock.*

Margaret *is a thin woman of fifty-four. She is wearing stout shoes, a skirt and a blouse, and a cotton shawl around her shoulders.*

Margaret *puts her darning into the workbasket and stands up.*

Nikolai *enters with* **Eileen** *and* **Matty**. **Matty** *has a new rucksack on his back.* **Nikolai** *is carrying a case.*

Nikolai *is a small, thin, wiry, light-haired boy of fourteen. He speaks almost faultless English. He is wearing his school uniform with the red scarf of the Young Pioneers.*

Matty *is wearing walking boots and a new, bright, expensive anorak.* **Eileen** *is wearing stout shoes and a heavy coat.*

Margaret *walks out of the garden to meet them on the muddy lane.*

Margaret Welcome to Brukin Bor.

Nikolai I would like you to meet my mother.

Margaret You must be Eileen.

Margaret *and* **Eileen** *shake hands.*

And Matty.

Matty Yes.

Margaret *and* **Matty** *shake hands.*

Margaret Welcome.

Matty Thank you very much.

Margaret It's such a pleasure to have you come and visit us.

Matty It's wonderful to be here.

Margaret Nikolai's been meeting every bus for the last two days.

Nikolai I am the talk of my school.

Margaret You are, aren't you?

Nikolai Yes.

Margaret (*to* **Eileen**, *smiling*) I'm not a real English person. His schoolfriends are terribly impressed. I hope he wasn't too effusive at the bus-stop?

Eileen No, he was lovely.

Matty He recognised us straight away.

Margaret Come through into the garden.

They go through the opening.

Margaret *takes the case from* **Nikolai.**

Why don't you take Matty to the den.

Nikolai Come. Come with me.

Margaret Wait a minute, let me explain first. My

husband has an office and, if you don't mind, I'd like you to share that with Nikolai?

Matty Yes.

Margaret We've put two campbeds there, and a little chest for your clothes.

Matty I can keep them in my rucksack.

Margaret That's up to you. Nikolai will help sort you out. It's not very far, but there's no water. So when you want a shower, or to wash at night, you'll have to do that here.

Matty Yes.

Margaret There's a stove, so you'll be nice and cosy. And I've told Nikolai that I don't want you staying up all night. It's all right to chat for half an hour, but after that I think it should be sleep.

Matty Yes.

Margaret Off you go the pair of you.

Nikolai Come with me, Matty.

Nikolai *and* **Matty** *go.*

Margaret *and* **Eileen** *smile at one another.*

Margaret I've put you in Nikolai's room.

Eileen You mustn't let us be a nuisance.

Margaret No, he's been longing to sleep in the den. You must know what growing boys are?

Eileen *smiles.*

Would you like to have a wash? And I'll show you his bed.

Eileen In a minute.

Margaret *smiles.*

Margaret Would you like a few moments on your own?

Eileen Yes, please.

Margaret I'll take your case in. Do come and find me when you're ready.

Eileen Thank you.

Margaret *goes into the house.*

A pause.

Eileen *follows her in.*

Margaret *returns. She is carrying a wooden chair which she puts down. She waits.*

Eileen *enters. She has her coat over her arm.*

Margaret If you don't mind he'll just need to pop in last thing at night.

Eileen *smiles.*

Eileen He can come in whenever 'e wants.

Margaret I won't have him doing that.

Eileen Is he your only child?

Margaret No, we've two who are grown up. They're both well into their twenties now. Nikolai was rather a surprise.

Eileen Do the others come home?

Margaret Yes. As often as they can. Edvard works at Bratsk in Siberia so it's sometimes quite difficult. But when they do, they sleep in the den. My daughter's in Leningrad.

Eileen Is it easier for her?

Margaret Yes, she gets a train to Moscow. And then like you, a train from Moscow, and then the bus. Whereas Edvard only receives one aeroplane ticket a year. I write every week. Nikolai wants to be like his elder brother in the den. He'll only be popping in for underclothes and socks.

Eileen I don't mind at all.

Margaret *smiles.*

Margaret My husband is still in America. I haven't any firm news. He agreed to telephone when he was sure he'd at least one fertile egg. I hope you can bear the uncertainty.

Eileen Yes.

Margaret I'm having to remind Nikolai there is a chance there won't be any. How would Matty react if that happened?

Eileen He'd be disappointed.

Margaret Would he?

Eileen He's his heart set on seeing them. Matty's ever an optimist. You can't knock him down.

Margaret *smiles.*

Margaret He's like my husband. He's travelled to America with such high hopes.

Eileen Are you worried?

Margaret I know how vulnerable children are.

Eileen Don't worry on Matty's account.

Margaret Matty's being here is very important to Pavel.

Eileen Is it?

Margaret He's set great store by your both coming.

Eileen It's important t'me. I feel humbled as a matter of fact. Mebbe it's important t'say jus' now how grateful we are. Matty thinks it, but 'e might forget.

Margaret Is he an independent boy?

Eileen I have thought it's uncanny – in Moscow he hardly put a foot wrong. How he knew where we were going I'll never know. I kept looking at him and thinking: well, 'e could be Russian, he's so good at this. The only thing 'e didn't manage was rooms side by side in the hotel. But he tried.

She smiles.

I've been coming to the conclusion that the world is a small place to 'im. He either doesn't know how big the world is, or he doesn't care. Don't get me wrong, I think it's marvellous that he can get us here.

Margaret Is he as bright at school?

Eileen I'm told he is. He doesn't concentrate like 'e should. But children don't these days, do they? He's like a frog from one thing t'the other. You say that, yet he manages himself so well.

A slight pause.

What happens if there aren't any fertile eggs?

Margaret My husband will try again next year.

Eileen Do your other two children take an interest?

Margaret Yes, very much so.

Eileen It's good when families can do that, isn't it?

Margaret *indicates a chair.*

Margaret Nikolai is growing up with all this excitement surrounding him, so it's rather different. Edvard and Rafiya didn't see their father travelling abroad. Nikolai is very special to my husband. He calls him our little miracle.

Eileen *sits in the chair and puts her coat over her lap.*

Eileen Children are miracles, aren't they?

Margaret I'm very impressed with Matty.

Margaret *sits.*

Eileen In Moscow I had to keep saying: pinch me, pinch me. I have never in my life seen so many people. You just get carried along with them, don't you?

Margaret A great deal of the excitement is the preparation for May Day, which is on Friday.

Eileen Is that what all the red is for?

Margaret *smiles.*

Margaret You are here at an interesting time.

Eileen *smiles.*

Eileen You know, the biggest shock was to see ordinary people going about their business. Getting onto trains, going to work. Getting into trams, coming home again. I know I must be ridiculous, am I?

Margaret *smiles.*

And everything in Moscow is so massive, isn't it?

Margaret Yes, it is.

Eileen It was like having a telescope in front of my eyes. It was all closer for me. Mebbe that's daft?

Margaret No.

Eileen D'you like living here?

Margaret I like the Oka reserve. I'm not a Moscow person, no.

Eileen You have the space, don't you?

Margaret Yes.

A slight pause.

I enjoyed Tunbridge Wells. The journeys in the car. On Sunday. With my parents. When I was in my teens.

Margaret *smiles.*

That life ended when I didn't choose to fall in love.

Eileen Didn't you?

Margaret Love finds us, I suspect. It found me in a very odd place. At first I was terribly reticent.

Eileen Yes.

Margaret Not unlike you, perhaps? I don't know. I felt this country was very different from my own.

A slight pause.

Eileen We didn't fall in love like that. It's good to see a woman who doesn't have regrets. You don't, do you?

Margaret No.

Eileen I married Jolly to get away from my mother. She was a tartar. I thought if we married I could live with his family.

Margaret Did you?

Eileen Yes. It was easy, you see, because I told Jolly I was pregnant by him. In actual fact it was another boy, it wasn't Jolly at all. Up until just now, I've always kept that to myself.

A slight pause.

Mebbe what I'm trying t'say is that I've done these things – yet I've criticised them in others. When your husband said I could come, I thought to myself: this is a new start, Eileen. Jolly was a great one for new starts. He would often say: let's put the past behind us. I was a girl in the shirt factory when we met. He washed his hands before opening a book did Jolly. It was his care for everything. It made me feel very stupid at times. I still wonder if I've underestimated myself?

A slight pause.

Mebbe what I'm trying to say is – if I hadn't underestimated myself, Jolly would never have underestimated his-self. I think that's what marriage is sometimes.

A telephone rings in the house.

Margaret I shan't be a moment.

Margaret *stands.*

Eileen Could it be America ringing?

Margaret Yes, it could.

Eileen I'll cross my fingers for you.

Margaret Do, please. Do cross your fingers.

Eileen *stands up.*

Eileen (*showing her*) Look.

Margaret We don't receive many calls. This might well be him at last.

Margaret *goes into the house.*

Nikolai and **Matty** *enter along the muddy lane.* **Matty** *is without his rucksack.*

Nikolai Is that my father telephoning?

Eileen I think so. Isn't it exciting?

Nikolai Yes. It will mean we shall have the White Crane at Oka.

Nikolai and **Matty** *enter the garden.*

The telephone stops ringing.

I would like to ask you if you receive telephone calls

from America, too?

Matty Erm, it depends if you know someone.

Nikolai When you are there did you make friends with American children?

Matty Not really, Nikolai.

Nikolai Was this forbidden by the leaders of your group?

Matty No, because I went with my mother. My mother was thinking of emigrating there, but she soon changed her mind.

Nikolai Emigrating?

Matty Yes.

Nikolai Like my own mother?

Matty That's right.

Nikolai My mother loved the Soviet Union a great deal. I must go to her.

Nikolai *runs towards the door.* **Margaret** *enters from the house. They very nearly collide.*

Margaret Be careful, Nikolai.

Nikolai *picks himself up.*

You heard the telephone ringing, didn't you?

Nikolai Yes?

Margaret It wasn't Daddy, unfortunately.

Nikolai (*pulling a face*) Oh.

Margaret *puts her arm around* **Nikolai**'s *shoulders.*

Margaret It was from the police. I'd forgotten, I have to take you to register with them. I've said we'll go this evening.

Nikolai Why have they been naughty already?

Margaret They haven't. It's something every visitor must do.

Nikolai *wriggles free of his mother's arm. He looks up at her.*

Nikolai Mummy, Daddy will ring us from America, won't he?

Margaret I hope so.

Nikolai I have told Matty he definitely will.

Margaret And I've told you it's not certain, haven't I?

Nikolai Yes.

Margaret I'm sorry, Matty, it isn't certain.

Matty No.

Margaret And Nikolai knows that. (*Looking him in the eye.*) It's very stupid, isn't it, to go getting yourself built up.

Nikolai Yes.

Margaret What happens when you do?

Nikolai I find myself disappointed.

Margaret Exactly.

Nikolai But, Mummy, he will ring, won't he?

Margaret Nikolai, because you want something, it doesn't mean it happens, does it?

Nikolai No. But, Mummy, he will ring, won't he?

Eileen Of course he'll ring, pet.

Nikolai *looks at* **Eileen**.

Margaret (*to* **Eileen**) He might not. (*To* **Nikolai**.) I know you want it so much.

Margaret *puts her arm around* **Nikolai**'*s shoulders.*

Nikolai I thought it might be Daddy on the telephone.

Margaret It wasn't, was it?

Nikolai No, it was the police for Matty.

Margaret Have you helped sort him out?

Nikolai (*brighter*) Yes.

Margaret Have you camped before, Matty?

Matty Erm – yes, I have. Well, rather, I've been youth hostelling once or twice.

Margaret That's what I used to do, to and from college, when I was a student. Did you enjoy it?

Matty Well, quite.

Margaret Not much?

Matty Not really.

Margaret It was a necessity for me. It was a way of travelling. I bicycled to and from college.

Matty Were you at university?

Margaret I was at teacher training in Cambridge.

Nikolai *wriggles free of his mother's arm.*

Nikolai Mummy, what is youth hostelling?

Matty (*going to him*) It's a lot of smelly feet, Nikolai.

Eileen No, it's not, don't confuse him.

Margaret It's a way of having a cheap holiday. People who like the countryside and who haven't a car, or who can't afford expensive train fares – they go youth hostelling. Don't they?

Matty Sometimes.

Nikolai Is it like a hotel?

Matty Well, not really.

Margaret It's like a very cheap hotel, isn't it?

Matty Yes.

Margaret Everyone sleeps in a dormitory, and in the morning you help with the chores, like washing-up, and sweeping, and clearing the leaves in the garden. It's very popular with English people.

Nikolai Were you organised by the leaders of your group?

Matty Well, I went with two friends.

Nikolai Is it like my Young Pioneers?

Margaret It's similar in that people share a comradeship, yes.

Nikolai I think I understand.

Margaret You don't actually, Nikolai.

Nikolai I do, Mummy.

Margaret *puts her arm around* **Nikolai***'s shoulders.*

Margaret He finds the concept of doing something on his own a very difficult one.

Nikolai (*looking up at her*) Why?

Margaret What did Matty just say?

Nikolai *wriggles free.*

Nikolai Were your two friends children like me?

Matty Yes.

Nikolai Did you elect a leader between you?

Matty No.

Nikolai But what if there was a squabble?

Matty Well, there was, that was the problem. We bickered all the time.

Nikolai We bicker, too, at my Young Pioneer Palace.

Matty What's that?

Margaret It's similar to the scouts. Every summer boys and girls go to a Young Pioneer camp. Don't you?

Nikolai Yes. For our holiday together.

Margaret I know you all sleep in dormitories, but it isn't like a youth hostel. Matty went on his own.

Nikolai Matty is more responsible than me?

Margaret *puts her arm around* **Nikolai**'s *shoulders.*

Margaret It's so hard to explain.

Nikolai Yes, it is.

He wriggles free.

Mummy, Matty went on holiday on his own, didn't he?

Margaret Yes.

Nikolai There were no leaders in his small group?

Margaret That's right.

Nikolai Mummy, when will I be an independent boy like Matty?

Margaret You do understand, don't you?

Nikolai Daddy has told me.

Margaret Has he?

Nikolai Yes.

Margaret I wonder if Daddy shouldn't be more careful.

Eileen He's independent now, aren't you?

Nikolai No.

Margaret I feel sure Matty would like a wash?

Matty I'm not very dirty.

Margaret Why don't you go and show him where the bathroom is.

Nikolai Come with me, Matty.

Nikolai *and* **Matty** *go into the house.*

Eileen His English is astonishing.

Margaret Yes, he has rather a rough ride at school. He's much better than his teacher, and she knows it. It has been quite a sticky problem, actually.

Eileen I can imagine.

Margaret He did make the mistake of correcting her. He's had to learn. He sits at his homework thinking of ways to say sentences badly.

Eileen Did you teach him from a baby?

Margaret No, not at all. He began at school with everyone else. It was Pavel who persuaded me it was churlish to sit back and pretend I couldn't help him. My children are inevitably a little different. Their friends are intrigued. Occasionally suspicious. Particularly their parents. I've tried to be quite quiet with Nikolai. I had the older children do French. It's difficult now because he thinks in English. He's streets ahead of the other children.

Eileen Are you worried?

Margaret No. Not quite. I think I may be though. Pavel pushes him a great deal.

Eileen At school?

Margaret At school and at home. I don't want to see him hurt, Eileen.

Eileen I know what yer mean. We were just the same with ours. I worried myself t'death sometimes.

Needlessly. Yet children will be what they'll be, won't they? Despite our wishes. Our fears. I've come to the conclusion that all yer can be is as selfless as you can.

Margaret *smiles.*

Nikolai *enters. He stops.*

Margaret You're not interrupting us. What is it?

Nikolai (*going to her*) Mummy, when Matty is finished, may I take him to see the Demoiselle Cranes?

Margaret Of course you may.

Eileen What are they?

Nikolai It is a crane which is only a little like the Siberian.

Margaret They're in paddocks.

Nikolai Yes, in enclosures. We can walk there.

Eileen Matty will like that.

Nikolai Mummy, when we have seen the Demoiselle Cranes, may I take Matty swimming?

Margaret No, it's too cold.

Nikolai I have my bathing costume.

Margaret I've said it's too cold, Nikolai.

Nikolai Yes.

A slight pause.

May I then take him to see the white-naped Crane?

Margaret You can do that.

Nikolai I would like to go on my bicycle.

Margaret Matty may borrow mine.

Nikolai Mummy, may we call on Dmitri?

Margaret No.

Nikolai He was thinking of going swimming this afternoon.

Margaret Nikolai, you won't be going anywhere if you carry on like this.

Nikolai Yes.

Matty *enters.*

Margaret I'm sorry, Matty, I don't want you messing about in the river. It still has ice in it.

Matty He said his friends will be there.

Margaret His friends can wait for a few days.

Matty *joins them.*

I'd like you to settle in first.

Matty I don't mind.

Margaret We'll see about swimming later. What I may do is ask Nikolai to invite his friends here.

Nikolai Dmitri wants to ask Matty something.

Margaret I bet he does. Dmitri's a ruffian. I don't like you playing with him.

Nikolai He set fire to the red flags.

Margaret I know he did. He's lucky to be alive.

Nikolai He's only alive because he is the policeman's son.

Margaret Not quite. Dmitri's eleven, Matty. He has a winning smile. You know that, don't you, Nikolai?

Nikolai Yes.

Margaret When he gets you running about for him?

Nikolai Yes.

Nikolai *shrugs.*

But I cannot help it. Little Dmitri is infectious.

Margaret He's heading for trouble. I don't want you playing with him while Matty's here. You're far too old for him.

Nikolai Yes.

A slight pause.

Mummy, may I have all my other friends come and meet Matty?

Margaret Yes, you may. I'm only asking to know where you are.

Nikolai Yes.

Margaret Be grown up.

Nikolai Yes.

A slight pause.

We are going to see the Demoiselle, and the White-naped Cranes. Come with me, Matty.

Margaret Have a good time both of you.

Nikolai *and* **Matty** *go.*

Eileen *puts her coat on.*

Would you like to go inside?

Eileen No, I don't mind.

Margaret This is almost the first day of spring. It still gets very cold in the evening.

A slight pause.

Eileen Were you a teacher at home?

Margaret I taught with my father for a year. He was the headmaster of a tiny Quaker school in Tunbridge Wells.

Eileen D'you see anything of him?

Margaret No, nothing at all. In fact, both my parents died some years ago.

Eileen *sits.*

When I married I became a Soviet citizen.

Eileen Did you miss England?

Margaret I still do, to some extent. Its gentility and refinement. It was obviously a big move to fall in love.

Margaret *sits.*

I miss the silly things, like the run to Brighton in the car.

Eileen Have you taught over here?

Margaret Occasionally, yes. It still isn't easy to be completely accepted. Even now people will be suspicious from time to time. I'm Pavel's secretary, really. Oka's a large reserve, much of it wild and forested. At the moment thousands of acres are underwater with the melting ice.

Eileen It can't be easy.

Margaret No, but that's what makes it exciting. My husband has assistance from the foresters.

She smiles.

I was, and still am, a Marxist. Much to my father's chagrin.

Eileen Was he upset?

Margaret Oh, he thought me naive. We wrote regularly.

Eileen It's not the same though, is it?

Margaret No. It was very difficult for them. Especially when we began a family.

Eileen Was it difficult for you?

Margaret Yes, it was quite. It's taken a long time to remove those suspicions. I was on my own with Edvard. Everywhere I went people hid their gaze. But children are children. His going to kindergarten helped a great deal.

She smiles.

I miss the teas on the lawn, and lemonade. I even miss the school with the children playing cricket. My father was a lifelong pacifist.

Eileen Was he?

Margaret My whole family were.

Eileen Jolly believed in pacifism. He used to say that wars were only a temporary solution.

Margaret *smiles.*

Margaret We sent photographs of the children. He was a brave man. In many ways Pavel is not unlike him. My grandfather was shot in the Great War, by a firing squad, for refusing to fight.

Eileen There's so much violence about, isn't there?

Margaret He'd said he could never kill. It helped me think about justice.

Eileen I argued with Jolly. I wasn't sure.

Margaret I first came here as a student. To a youth festival in Moscow. When I first met Pavel he wanted to know about rock-'n'-roll and Teddy-boys. I was almost the last person to ask. I saw these young men with cardboard guitars, and one record, which they mimed to unceasingly.

Eileen You weren't a rock-'n'-roller?

Margaret I was playing with an orchestra.

Eileen D'you still?

Margaret Only periodically. We've tried to interest Nikolai, but he isn't keen. I don't believe you should force children. He much prefers the outdoors.

Eileen *fastens her coat.*

Why don't I take you in?

Eileen In a minute. I'm quite happy.

Margaret My grandfather was a good musician. I'm told he was.

Eileen It's awful what people will do to each other, isn't it?

Margaret Yes.

Eileen Did you come back to meet your husband?

Margaret We weren't married then. I was eager to see Moscow for myself, if I could, away from the group. By then I'd finished college and was busily teaching.

She picks up the sock from the workbasket and puts it on her lap.

I never meant to stay. I didn't even bring my cello. At the bottom of my bag I had Jerry Lee Lewis, and Little Richard. Rafiya still plays them.

Eileen Were they Pavel's favourites?

Margaret I can't really remember, Eileen. I think so, yes. Like most young people we were growing up.

She begins to darn the sock.

In fact, in a funny way, I think it was my father who knew I was coming here forever. He kept asking why I wasn't taking the cello.

Eileen What did your grandfather play?

Margaret The piano. There is a natural way of things; a course of justice which is right for one person and not another.

Eileen Your grandfather was brave.

Margaret Very, I think. Pavel was, too. And his sister. We met at his sister's flat. It was difficult then to meet a Russian, in a Russian home.

Margaret *smiles.*

Eileen Can I help you?

Margaret No, don't be silly.

Eileen It's years since I darned.

Margaret Is it?

Eileen My goodness I used to.

Margaret I wouldn't miss darning.

Eileen You didn't see your father again?

Margaret No, unfortunately.

Eileen There is a price for whatever we do, isn't there?

Margaret Yes, I think there is, very much so.

Eileen If we're not careful criticism comes very cheap.

Margaret *smiles.*

Eileen I wish Jolly was here.

Margaret Do you?

Eileen Yes, I do.

Margaret I wasn't at all sure about your coming.

Eileen Weren't you? You shouldn't worry about us.

Margaret I don't worry. Well, I do. I worry about

Nikolai. I'm sure unnecessarily.

Eileen *smiles.*

Margaret *has finished darning. She snaps the wool between her fingers. She puts the wool and the needle in her workbasket. She takes a shirt from the bottom.*

Eileen You won't worry about us, will you?

Margaret No.

Eileen I know what you mean when you say there's a natural course of justice.

Margaret Do you?

Eileen Yes.

Margaret I wasn't doubting you.

Eileen I know you weren't.

Margaret *smiles.*

Margaret The pinnacle of our life here is Pavel's work with the cranes.

Eileen *holds up her crossed fingers.*

He's fought so tirelessly, and unselfishly. It has to work for him.

Eileen It will. Have you buttons to sew?

Margaret Yes.

Eileen Give it me.

Eileen *takes the shirt.*

Margaret Why don't I take you in?

Eileen In a minute. Unless you want to?

Margaret No.

Margaret *takes another shirt from the workbasket.*

Eileen I'm a dab hand at this.

Margaret We shouldn't be so long. I haven't even offered you tea.

The two women prepare to sew.

Scene Two

That night.

Pavel's small, wooden office which has a log-burning stove in one corner. Below the window is a desk, one side of which is crammed with files and papers. On the other side is an electric incubator. The desk also has a writing lamp, a telephone, and a swivel chair. Elsewhere is a bookcase untidily stuffed with periodicals and books.

The curtains are drawn. There are two campbeds, made up for the night, on the wooden floor. The writing lamp is on.

Nikolai *and* **Matty**. **Nikolai** *is wearing trousers, a jumper, and his red scarf.*

Nikolai This is the scarf of the Young Pioneers. Do you have a scarf, Matty?

Matty No.

Nikolai When I am older I shall join the Komsomol, which is the Communist Union of Youth. At your school, what do they do when you are naughty?

Matty Erm – we get lines and extra prep.

Nikolai What is prep?

Matty Extra homework.

Nikolai And lines?

Matty Lines are completely ridiculous, Nikolai. Absolutely bloody pointless. They're given to demean us.

Nikolai Why?

Matty A good question. We have to write out hundreds of times what we've done wrong.

Nikolai When you are naughty?

Matty Yes.

Nikolai Please may I ask you – are you often naughty at your school?

Matty Well – sometimes. It isn't quite like that though, not in the sixth form.

Nikolai At my school they take away our scarfs. You will not inform my mother?

Matty No.

Nikolai My scarf keeps on disappearing for being naughty.

There is a knock on the wooden door.

Nikolai *and* **Matty** *look towards it.*

(*Quietly.*) Oh dear, oh dear. We must hide. Quickly. We must get under the covers.

Nikolai *and* **Matty** *jump into their beds. They pull the blankets up to their necks.*

Matty (*quietly*) Who is it?

The door opens.

Margaret *enters.*

Margaret Are you both comfortable?

Matty Yes.

Nikolai Yes, thank you, Mummy.

Margaret Have you plenty of logs?

Nikolai Yes, Matty helped me to carry some.

Margaret Good. I've some news for you. Daddy's here.

Nikolai Daddy is here?

Nikolai *jumps out of bed.*

Margaret Nikolai Pavlovich, why aren't you in your pyjamas?

Nikolai Mummy, we, er –

A slight pause.

Margaret What did I say, Nikolai?

Nikolai Yes.

Matty *gets out of bed.*

Matty It's my fault.

Margaret Why aren't you in your pyjamas, Matty?

Nikolai We were searching for his pyjamas. They've run away somewhere.

Margaret Don't be silly.

Nikolai Yes, Mummy, they have. Gone. (*Looking at him.*) Where to, Matty?

Margaret *looks at* **Matty**.

Matty We were only talking.

Margaret Matty's more sense, hasn't he? I sometimes think you've not got the brains you were born with, Nikolai.

Nikolai Pardon?

Margaret As it happens, it doesn't matter. I came to tell you to get dressed. Now, listen to me, Daddy's very tired. He's had a long journey from America.

Nikolai But, Mummy, he has not telephoned us?

Margaret I know. He's tried, and couldn't get through.

Nikolai (*disappointed*) He has no eggs for us.

Margaret *puts her arm around* **Nikolai**'s *shoulders.*

Margaret Look at me, Nikolai.

Nikolai *looks up at her.*

Nikolai Please, Mummy?

Margaret He's three eggs. One has unfortunately died on the journey.

Nikolai Three eggs?

Margaret Yes. Two are still alive.

Nikolai Two eggs. We shall have the White Crane at Oka?

Margaret Yes.

Nikolai I must go and find my Daddy, mustn't I?

Margaret No, he's coming here.

Nikolai But my Daddy needs me.

Pavel *enters. He is carrying a large portable incubator.*

Nikolai *rushes towards him.*

Pavel Careful.

Eileen *follows* **Pavel** *in.*

Pavel *puts his arm around* **Nikolai**'s *shoulders.*

You were dressed quickly.

Nikolai We were not undressed, Daddy.

Pavel Hello.

Matty (*suddenly shyly*) Hello.

Pavel What do you think of our country?

Matty It's great.

Pavel (*to* **Nikolai**) You two have made good friends?

Nikolai Yes.

Pavel (*to* **Matty**) All boys must talk, I think. It is very good you talk. (*To* **Nikolai**.) When I am a student we stay awake all those nights.

Nikolai Did you?

Pavel Of course. I was a little older than you, but – well, what does it matter?

Margaret Pavel.

Pavel Yes, your Mummy is right as usual. I am very tired. I have come a long way today.

Nikolai Please, Daddy, please may I see the eggs?

Pavel Of course.

Nikolai Thank you.

Matty May I, please?

Pavel Of course. Both of you.

Pavel *puts the incubator on the floor.*

I must remind you to be very, very careful. These are very precious.

Nikolai Me first.

Nikolai *kneels by the incubator.*

Margaret Nikolai.

Nikolai What, Mummy?

Margaret Don't overstep the mark.

Nikolai No.

Matty *kneels by the incubator.*

Matty What's happened to the one which has died?

Pavel *kneels.*

Pavel I do not know yet. I will have to look into it. Tomorrow.

Nikolai Me first.

Margaret Nikolai Pavlovich.

Nikolai (*looking up at her, shamefaced*) What?

Margaret Stand up.

Nikolai *stands up.*

Eileen He's only excited.

Margaret One more word out of you and a rocket will go up. Is that absolutely clear?

Nikolai Yes.

A slight pause.

May I kneel again?

Margaret Yes.

Nikolai *kneels.*

Pavel (*to* **Nikolai**) Has the electricity been put into the incubator?

Nikolai *looks at his mother.*

Margaret Nikolai's had it plugged in since the day you left.

Pavel I do not want them to get cold, you understand. This is what I have striven for, for ten years.

Pavel *lifts the hinged lid of the incubator, revealed in a compartment at the top are three crane eggs.*

They look at them.

Matty Which is the dead one?

Pavel This one.

Matty Can I lift it out?

Pavel Yes.

Matty *lifts it out.*

Matty (*to* **Eileen**) It's heavier than the ones Jolly had.

Pavel It has a chick inside it. Unfortunately, you know sometimes there is a weakness.

Matty It's still warm.

Pavel It is in the incubator - so, yes.

Matty *puts the egg back.*

Matty These are the live ones?

Pavel Be very careful, please.

Matty *lifts up a live egg.*

Only for a very short moment. You like?

Matty Yes.

Pavel Inside is a little Siberian Crane chick for Oka. Please put him down now.

Matty *returns the egg to the incubator.*

You would like to listen to him?

Matty Yes.

Pavel You will hear he is alive in there.

Pavel *takes a stethoscope from the pocket of his suit jacket.*

Matty *puts the stethoscope on. He listens.*

You hear him?

Matty Eh, you can, it's absolutely brilliant.

Pavel He is moving about in there, just a little bit.

Matty *continues to listen.*

Eileen Matty, give Nikolai a go.

Matty In a minute. I haven't finished yet.

Pavel Just for one more moment, and then for my son.

A pause.

Eileen Matty.

Matty What are they doing when they're moving about?

Pavel It is important they do not settle, you know.

Nikolai Daddy, in the wild the mother bird turns the egg, doesn't she?

Pavel Of course. We must turn the eggs, too. Every two hours we must do that.

Nikolai Daddy, the embryo is delicate, isn't it?

Pavel Until the nest of the Grey Crane we must be his mother. You are right, Nikolai. Until the cuckoo.

He taps **Matty** *on the shoulder.*

I think for my son now, please.

Matty *looks up. He takes the stethoscope off and gives it to* **Nikolai**.

Nikolai *stands up.*

Nikolai Would you like to listen?

Eileen No, no, no, it's your turn.

Nikolai *kneels. He puts the stethoscope on and listens to the eggs.*

Margaret *comes up behind him and leans over.*

Margaret Can you hear them?

Nikolai Yes. It is like a little rustling.

Margaret Nikolai's heard them before, Matty.

Nikolai Not the Siberian egg.

Margaret No, but similar. The Demoiselle Crane, and the White-naped Crane. (*Looking at him.*) Bed, Pavel.

Pavel We must put the eggs into the incubator now.

Nikolai May I?

Pavel Yes.

Nikolai *stands up. He opens the lid of the other incubator. He transfers one of the live eggs.*

Nikolai I should turn the egg over, too?

Pavel Yes.

Nikolai *turns the egg.*

Margaret They're not going to get any sleep, are they?

Pavel Not tonight. They must do this.

Nikolai *transfers the other live egg.*

Margaret I wonder if I shouldn't stay here?

Pavel They will be fine.

Margaret Why don't we take the incubator to our room?

Pavel It will be in the way. It is easier for them.

Nikolai *turns the egg.*

Matty *stands. He picks up the remaining egg. He gives it to* **Nikolai**.

Nikolai *looks at* **Pavel**.

In there, yes, until the morning.

Nikolai *puts the egg into the incubator. He closes the lid.*

Eileen *goes to* **Matty**.

Eileen (*quietly*) No fooling about.

Matty No.

Eileen You know what a responsibility this is, don't you?

Matty Yes.

Margaret Do you, Matty?

Matty Look – I'm not a child.

Nikolai *goes to* **Pavel**.

Nikolai Daddy, the incubator must stay at ninety-eight degrees?

Pavel Yes.

Margaret I'll come down at three o'clock and check you're both all right.

Pavel No, it is not necessary.

Margaret I'm coming down at three o'clock, Pavel.

Pavel No. There is the telephone. If there is a problem they will pick it up and they will ring. My son will do this.

Margaret Are you sure?

Pavel Of course.

Margaret *smiles and goes to* **Pavel**.

Margaret I hope you're right.

Pavel I am.

Margaret I'll take Eileen back. Don't be long, will you?

Pavel I will be one moment only.

Margaret *goes to* **Eileen**.

Eileen Good night.

Margaret *and* **Eileen** *go.*

Pavel *takes a small box from his pocket.*

Pavel I have this for you.

Nikolai *takes it.*

Nikolai What is it?

Pavel Open it and see.

Nikolai *opens the box.*

It is a very small pocket calculator. No batteries, no problems. It works by the sun.

Nikolai *is madly tapping on the keys.*

Matty It's a solar calculator.

Nikolai You have one?

Matty Yes.

Nikolai I have one, too, now.

Nikolai *trys to undo it.*

Matty What're you doing?

Nikolai I'm trying to take it apart to see how it works, Matty.

Pavel I will tell you in the morning.

Matty It doesn't come apart like that.

Nikolai Why?

Matty It just doesn't, that's all.

Nikolai Well, it should.

Matty You'll break it.

Nikolai *stops.*

Nikolai Daddy, how does it work from the sun?

Pavel *ruffles* **Nikolai**'s *hair.*

Pavel It has a photo-electric cell. You are a jack-in-the-box tonight. Too many questions. I will explain it all in the morning. I must go.

Pavel *goes. The door closes behind him.*

Matty I can tell you how it works, Nikolai.

Scene Three

The office. A bright, spring morning, two days later.

The curtains are drawn and the door is open. On each of the campbeds is an anorak and a rucksack.

Pavel, **Nikolai**, **Matty**, **Margaret** *and* **Eileen**. **Nikolai** *is wearing wellingtons, and* **Matty** *has walking boots.*

Pavel *is by the electric incubator. He opens it and very carefully he transfers one of the live eggs to a small portable incubator.*

The others watch.

Pavel *transfers the second egg. He closes and fastens the lid of the portable incubator. He turns the electric incubator off at the plug.*

Nikolai *and* **Matty** *go to their anoraks. They put them on.* **Nikolai**'s *anorak is not as bright, and is a much poorer quality than* **Matty**'s.

Margaret *goes to* **Nikolai**. *She helps him. She does up the zip at the front.*

Matty *does his own zip.* **Eileen** *watches.*

Nikolai *and* **Matty** *put their rucksacks on their backs. They jiggle up and down to get them comfortable.*

The others watch.

Pavel *goes to* **Nikolai** *and ruffles his hair.* **Nikolai** *beams.*

Matty *smiles at* **Eileen.** **Eileen** *smiles, and then looks down for a second.*

Nikolai *goes to the portable incubator and picks it up by the handle.*

Pavel *watches.*

Matty *joins* **Nikolai.** *They go out through the door.*

A slight pause.

Margaret *turns to* **Pavel.**

Margaret It's such a long way.

Pavel Sometimes, I think, we must journey for ourselves.

He turns to **Eileen.**

Jolly, he would have given the eggs to the boys, dear lady?

Eileen Yes, he would.

Margaret *goes to* **Pavel.** *She runs her hand across his stomach.* **Pavel** *puts his arm around her.* **Margaret** *kisses him once on the lips.*

The three adults are still.

Scene Four

Later that morning.

The vast Oka forest which is submerged in water and melting snow. The hundreds of silver birch trees still have no leaves, and they look almost barren as they twist and turn from the flood water towards the sky.

A cold, spring sunlight.

There is a tiny island which the flooding has left. The grass is rough and dead. A silver birch is growing.

On the flood water is a boat with an outboard motor. The propeller is raised and has grass and twigs around it.

Nikolai and **Matty** *are in the boat.* **Matty** *is sitting in the bows.* **Nikolai** *is at the stern clearing the propeller.*

Nikolai It is another twenty kilometers to the Grey Crane's nest.

Matty Let me have a look.

He joins **Nikolai** *at the stern.*

Nikolai I can do it, thank you, Matty.

Matty You can't do everything. There's some things I'm better at than you. I know about boats.

Matty *leans out, beside* **Nikolai**, *towards the propeller.*

Nikolai Please, you are pushing me away.

Matty It's you, you're absolutely, pathetically, useless.

Nikolai Pardon?

Matty If only you'd budge I'd have the space.

Nikolai *moves.*

Nikolai Matty, we should stop now.

Matty My brilliance is saving the day here, Nikolai.

Nikolai The water is too shallow.

Matty It's best if we go as far as we can in the boat. Don't you agree?

Nikolai *shrugs.*

Nikolai I have tried to tell you my thoughts.

Matty Doesn't it get deeper farther on?

Nikolai No, Matty, it doesn't. We are off the river now.

Matty Nurd, why didn't you say?

Nikolai Pardon? What is a nurd?

Matty Nothing. It's an expression of endearment.

Nikolai Matty, nurd, sometimes your ears are blind to what I have to say.

Matty You sound just like your mother.

Nikolai Mummy. Why?

Matty She's a nurd if ever there was one.

Nikolai *smiles.*

Nikolai You like my mother? I love her, too.

Nikolai *steps out of the boat into the shallow flood water.*

Please may I ask you – I would like to ask if all mothers are as strict in England?

Matty *leaves the propeller and sits in the boat.*

Matty Well, not really. It depends. Some are.

Nikolai Is yours, Matty?

Matty No.

Nikolai *picks up the incubator and carries it towards the island.*

Nikolai My friends at school, their mothers are not as strict as mine.

Matty You know what I think?

Nikolai No?

Matty Well, you have to educate your parents.

Nikolai Pardon?

Matty Put your foot down now and again.

Nikolai *puts the incubator down. He looks nonplussed. He walks back towards the boat.*

Nikolai Oh, I could never do that. It is wrong to insult our parents.

Matty You'll have to eventually.

Nikolai Why?

Matty If you want to grow up.

Nikolai Pardon, no, Matty. My parents have great respect for me.

Matty It doesn't get you very far though, does it?

Nikolai I do not like you insulting my mother. Nurd is not a nice word. You are a nurd.

Nikolai *picks up a rucksack and carries it towards the island.*

Matty Don't get upset.

Nikolai I am not upset. I do not like you when you think you are wonderful.

Matty I do, do I?

Nikolai Yes, you do.

Matty That's because I am, Nikolai.

Nikolai *puts the rucksack down.*

Nikolai No, you are a little boy like me.

He walks back to the boat.

Please, we have to shake hands now.

He offers his hand. **Matty** *hesitates.*

We must if I am to be your friend again.

The two boys shake hands.

Nikolai *pushes the boat, through the flood water, to the island.*

Matty *steps out of the boat.*

Please, would you fasten the rope to the tree.

Matty I'm not a dogsbody, Nikolai.

Nikolai Pardon?

Matty I'm not your slave.

A slight pause.

Nikolai *takes the painter from the bows of the boat.* **Matty** *pushes him away.*

Get off, I'm doing it.

Matty *takes the painter and fastens it to the tree.*

Nikolai *takes the rucksack from the boat and puts it with the other one and the incubator.*

The two boys look at one another. **Nikolai** *walks to* **Matty** *and offers his hand.*

What's the point of that if it makes no difference?

Nikolai In my country this is the way children say we are sorry to one another.

Matty Yes, well, I'm not sorry, and I'm not a child.

Nikolai When we shake hands we must honour what we have done.

Matty Yes, well you can fuck off.

Nikolai Pardon?

Matty Leave me alone. Okay?

Nikolai Yes.

Nikolai *walks to the rucksacks and the incubator.*

The two boys are silent for a moment.

Nikolai *walks to* **Matty** *offering his hand.*

Please, Matty, this is very wrong.

Matty What did I just say?

Nikolai Yes.

Nikolai *walks back to the rucksacks and the incubator.*

The two boys are silent for a moment.

Matty I'm in charge. Okay?

Nikolai Yes.

Matty *walks to the incubator and kneels down. He opens the lid.*

Nikolai *kneels.*

Are you going to turn them, Matty?

Matty *looks at his watch.*

Matty It's an hour and fifty minutes since we did them last.

Matty *turns both the eggs. He closes the lid and stands up. He begins to put his rucksack on.*

A slight pause.

Nikolai *stands up.*

Nikolai Excuse me, but you did not check the temperature.

Matty Well done, Nikolai.

Matty *has his rucksack on. He kneels by the incubator and opens the lid.*

It's ninety-seven degrees. That's within the limits, isn't it.

Nikolai *kneels.*

Nikolai No, Matty, it isn't.

Nikolai *leans over.* **Matty** *covers the thermometer with his hands.*

Matty Stop trying to look, I've read it correctly.

Nikolai *trys to move* **Matty***'s hands.*

Nikolai I must check, too, please.

Matty *pushes* **Nikolai** *away.* **Nikolai** *falls onto his back.* **Matty** *closes the incubator and stands up. He picks the incubator up by the handle.*

Nikolai *stands up.*

I am not going on with you. You are a spoilt baby.

Matty Well, you'll have to.

Nikolai No, not until we shake hands.

Matty The eggs will die then, won't they?

Silence.

Nikolai Please – please may I ask you to tell me what I have done wrong?

Matty Wrong?

Nikolai Yes.

A pause.

There were no leaders in your small group, Matty.

A slight pause.

I think you are a very unkind boy.

Matty *walks to the boat.*

Matty I'm going back the way we came.

Nikolai No, you will not find it on your own.

Matty Well, if you show me, Nikolai?

Nikolai I would have to see my father.

A slight pause.

Please, Matty, you must raise the temperature in the incubator.

A slight pause.

Matty Is it dangerously low?

Nikolai Yes, it is.

A slight pause.

Please, Matty, you must be as quick as you can.

A slight pause.

Please – please may I ask you why you want the eggs to die?

A slight pause.

May I show you?

A slight pause.

Matty *walks to* **Nikolai** *and puts the incubator down.* **Nikolai** *kneels and begins to undo the rucksack at his feet.* **Matty** *takes his rucksack off and puts it down.* **Nikolai** *stands up.*

You must find the pan and the gas-ring from the bottom of my rucksack.

Matty *kneels. He takes a portable gas-ring and a pan from* **Nikolai**'s *rucksack.*

You must take the hot-water bottle too now.

Matty *takes a rubber hot water-bottle from the rucksack. He looks up at* **Nikolai**.

Please empty the water into the pan.

Matty *unscrews the top of the hot-water bottle. He empties a small amount of water into the pan.* **Nikolai** *bends down and delves into his rucksack for matches. He gives them to* **Matty**. **Matty** *lights the gas. He puts the pan on.*

A slight pause.

Nikolai *kneels.*

A pause.

Matty Nikolai.

Matty *offers his hand.*

A slight pause.

Nikolai *shakes his head.*

Why not?

Nikolai Now we must wait for the water to be hot.

Matty *picks up the hot-water bottle and offers it to* **Nikolai**.

Matty Would you like to do it?

Nikolai *takes the hot-water bottle. He delves into his rucksack and takes out a Sony Walkman complete with headphones.*

Nikolai Do you have one of these, Matty?

Matty *undoes his rucksack. He takes out his Sony Walkman.*

Matty Yours is better than mine, it's the older version.

Nikolai Better?

Matty I had one, but I sold it.

Nikolai Daddy brought me mine from America. All my friends at school they love to put the headphones on, and hear the popular tapes.

Nikolai *puts the headphones on.*

We have a problem with batteries in our family.

Nikolai *presses the buttons on the cassette recorder.*

Look, it does not work.

He dances on his knees as if there was music playing.

Matty *opens his cassette-recorder and takes out the batteries.*

Matty Well, would you like mine?

Nikolai *stops dancing and takes the headphones off.*
He hesitates.

I'd like you to have them.

Nikolai *takes the calculator from a pocket in his anorak.*
He looks at it for a moment.

Nikolai Would you accept this?

Matty They're a present, Nikolai.

Nikolai Oh, dear.

Matty What's the matter?

Nikolai I must give you something in return.

Matty I don't want anything.

Nikolai Oh dear.

Matty They're yours.

Nikolai No, I could not do that.

Nikolai *stands up. He looks at the pan.*

May I do this please, Matty?

Matty Yes.

Nikolai *puts his calculator away. He turns the gas-ring off*
and begins to fill the hot-water bottle from the pan.

Matty *takes* **Nikolai**'s *Walkman and puts his batteries into it.*

Nikolai What are you doing?

Matty I'm giving you them.

Nikolai No, you must not.

Matty Well, I am. There.

Matty *puts* **Nikolai**'s *Walkman back.*

Nikolai *puts the pan down and screws the top on the hot-water bottle.*

Nikolai Now you must take the cold hot-water bottle from the incubator.

Matty *opens the small compartment at the bottom. He slides out another rubber hot-water bottle.* **Nikolai** *gives* **Matty** *the hot one,* **Matty** *gives* **Nikolai** *the cold one.* **Matty** *looks up at* **Nikolai.**

That's right, back in there.

Matty *slides the fresh hot water bottle into the compartment at the bottom of the incubator and closes it.*

Nikolai *kneels down.*

Matty, you must wait and see if this works now.

Matty *offers his hand.*

Nikolai *delves into an anorak pocket and finds a small badge.*

Would you accept this? It is not much. It is a small badge of Vladimir Lenin, which I have for swopping at school.

Matty Yes.

Matty *takes it. He pins it to his anorak.*

Nikolai You are like a Russian boy now.

Matty *offers his hand.*

Matty, I will not shake your hand until you tell me what I have done wrong?

A slight pause.

Matty Well, that's particularly difficult.

Nikolai Why?

Matty Nikolai, please, just shake my hand.

A slight pause.

You're hurting me.

Nikolai Why?

Matty You're hurting me, Nikolai.

Nikolai Please, Matty, tell me why I'm hurting you?

A slight pause.

Matty It's particularly difficult because you haven't done anything wrong.

A slight pause.

Nikolai I don't understand. Matty, I must know.

Matty It's not you, you idiot. It's me.

Nikolai Pardon?

Matty It's me.

A slight pause.

Nikolai Pardon?

Matty *offers his hand.*

Matty Look, just shake my hand before I die or something.

Nikolai You will not die.

Matty Oh, for fuck's sake.

Nikolai What is a fucks?

Matty Shake it, you bastard.

Nikolai What is a bastard?

Matty Shake it. Please.

Nikolai *shakes his hand.*

Thank you.

Silence.

Nikolai May I ask – what is a fucks and what is a bastards?

Matty They're swear-words. They're nothing.

Nikolai Like nurd?

Matty No, stronger than nurd.

Matty s*tands up. He picks up the incubator and carries it away a few feet. He puts it down and kneels.*

Nikolai *stands up.*

Nikolai May I ask you why you don't like my mother?

Matty I do. She's great.

Matty *opens the incubator.*

Nikolai You know, Matty, sometimes you are a boy who always wants his own way.

Nikolai *kneels. He packs up and fastens both the rucksacks.*

Matty *closes the incubator.*

Nikolai *stands up and gives* **Matty** *his rucksack.*

Matty *stands up.*

Please, what was the temperature?

Matty Ninety-eight-and-a-half degrees. That's right, isn't it?

Nikolai Yes, it is.

Matty *puts his rucksack on.* **Nikolai** *puts his on.*

Matty *picks up the incubator by the handle.*

Nikolai *walks past* **Matty** *and continues on the journey.*

Matty *follows him.*

Scene Five

Later.

The dense silver birches of the Oka forest. A large island which the flooding has left. The grass is thick and coarse, and wild with bulrushes. On the ground, between the trees, is a Grey Crane's nest made of twigs and brown grass.

A cold, evening sunlight.

Nikolai *enters. He looks towards the nest.*

Matty *enters. He stops. He puts the incubator down and sits on it.*

Nikolai Please do not sit on the incubator.

Matty *stands up.*

Nikolai *runs up the slight incline towards the nest, and kneels down beside it.*

Matty Is that it?

Nikolai *picks up a Grey Crane egg from the nest.*

Nikolai We are here at last, Matty.

Matty *runs up the incline to the nest. He kneels.*

Matty We've found it.

Nikolai Yes.

Matty *picks up an egg.*

Matty Where's the mother?

Nikolai Our footsteps will have frightened her away.

Nikolai *puts the Grey Crane egg back in the nest.*

Matty, we must not go on like this, you and me.

Matty *puts his egg back into the nest.*

Are you tired?

Matty Yes.

Nikolai I am exhausted by tiredness.

Matty Are you feeling all right?

Nikolai No, Matty, I am not. I am finding it all so very hard, my English and everything, and you.

Matty *looks down.*

This is not right between us.

Matty *looks up.*

Matty I'm sorry, Nikolai.

Nikolai *stands up.*

Nikolai You must be the cuckoo now.

Nikolai *walks to the incubator and carries it back to the nest. He puts it down and kneels.*

Please may I ask you – well, I would like to know if you are the same with your other friends?

Matty *takes his wristwatch off. He offers it to* **Nikolai.**

Nikolai *shows the wristwatch on his own arm.*

I do not need it, you know.

Matty Well, if I have anything, it's yours.

Matty *puts his wristwatch back on his arm.*

Nikolai There is one thing. Please may I ask – well, I would like to ask if you will speak to my mother for me?

Matty Yes.

Nikolai Matty, please may I visit you at your home near Middlesborough?

Matty Well, of course you may, you idiot.

Nikolai If I ask my mother she will only say 'no'. If you ask her, then I will chip in and be enthusiastic.

Matty Yes.

Nikolai I would love to meet your friends and see them
for myself.

A slight pause.

Matty Well, do you imagine they're all as bad as me?

Nikolai Is Britain a very different country from the
Soviet Union?

A slight pause.

Matty Yes, I think so.

Nikolai You are very lucky to come here.

A slight pause.

Matty I know you don't like me, Nikolai.

Nikolai I think you are a boy who always feels sorry for
himself, Matty.

Matty (*gently*) Do I?

Nikolai Yes, you do.

A slight pause.

Matty Do I seem self-pitying?

Nikolai Yes.

A slight pause.

Matty, we must be the cuckoo.

Nikolai *opens the incubator.*

You must pass me the eggs from the Grey Crane nest.

Matty *picks up a Grey Crane egg and gives it to* **Nikolai**.
Nikolai *puts it in the incubator.*

The mother will not be far away, we must be very quick.

Matty *quickly picks up two more eggs from the Grey Crane's nest.*

Without being slapdash, Matty.

Matty *slows down. He gives them to* **Nikolai**. **Nikolai** *puts them into the incubator.*

Now you must find the artificial egg from your rucksack.

Matty *takes off his rucksack. He opens it and finds the pot egg. He gives it to* **Nikolai**. **Nikolai** *puts it in the nest.*

Now, please, you must pass me, very carefully, the fertile eggs of the White Siberian Crane.

Matty *carefully picks up one of the Siberian Crane eggs. He holds it in his left hand.*

A slight pause.

He offers his right hand to **Nikolai**.

A slight pause.

Matty Why not?

Nikolai Matty, I have let you do everything, haven't I?

Matty Please, Nikolai.

Nikolai *stands up. He moves away. He stops.*

Nikolai I will come over here, if that is what you want?

A slight pause.

Look, I am over here.

A slight pause.

They will get cold and the mother will never come back.

A slight pause.

Look, Matty.

Matty *stands up. He offers his hand.*

Matty Why not, Nikolai?

Nikolai *hesitates.*

Please.

Nikolai We should go home now, I think.

Matty *has the egg in his hand.*

Matty, what else can I do?

Matty Just shake my hand.

A slight pause.

Nikolai *shakes his head.*

Nikolai No, you are a very naughty boy.

Matty *picks up the second Siberian Crane egg from the incubator. He presses his fingers around them.*

Matty I'll break them.

Nikolai No, Matty, you would not do that.

Matty I would.

Nikolai Matty, you are a nice boy really.

Matty *hits the two eggs together. The shells crack. The eggs break. The embryos come out into his hands.*

Silence.

Look what you have gone and done.

Silence.

You have gone and killed those eggs. How could you go and do that? I hate you.

Silence.

I hate you, I hate you, I hate you. I will kick you if you do not give those eggs to me.

Nikolai *goes to* **Matty.** *He cups his hands.* **Matty** *gives him* *the broken shells and the embryos.*

I will kick you if you do not get out of my sight.

Matty *moves away from the nest.*

If you come near me again I will kick you, and kick you, and kick you.

Nikolai *kneels.*

I wish you would get out of my sight I hate you so much.

Matty *moves away a few more feet.*

Nikolai *is looking at the embryos.*

Silence.

Matty Is it possible to rescue them?

Nikolai If you talk to me once more I will come over there and kick you.

Silence.

No, it is not possible, Matty.

Matty *has tears in his eyes.*

There's no need to cry as well, you horrible big baby.

Nikolai *puts the embryos in the grass.*

If you're going to cry, will you cry away from here.

Nikolai *fastens the incubator lid. He stands up. He picks up the incubator.*

I hate you, Matty.

Nikolai *goes.*

Matty *is still, with tears in his eyes.*

A pause.

He begins to sob. He goes to his rucksack and puts it on. He jiggles up and down to get it more comfortable.

Nikolai *enters. He stops.*

Matty *looks at him.*

Matty, I have decided I must return the Grey Crane eggs to the nest.

Matty May I help you?

Nikolai No. Please move away.

Matty *moves away from the nest.*

Nikolai *takes the incubator to the nest. He kneels.*

Matty I'm sorry, Nikolai.

Nikolai I think you are a boy who will always be sorry. I am sorry, too.

Nikolai *takes the pot egg from the nest. He stands up.*

I have decided I cannot leave you on your own.

He goes to **Matty**. *He puts the egg into the rucksack.*

You did not fasten this.

Matty Didn't I?

Nikolai No. Our belongings might have fallen out.

Nikolai *fastens the rucksack. He goes back to the nest. He kneels.*

Matty *goes to the nest.*

I do not want you near me.

Matty *kneels.*

I think you will always disagree with other people, Matty.

Matty If I tell your father, Nikolai.

A slight pause.

Nikolai I do not know what I must tell him.

Matty If I tell your father, will you tell my grandmother?
She'll kill me.

Nikolai Kill you? Like you killed the Siberian eggs? I do
not think your grandmother will kill you, Matty.

A slight pause.

This was my father's big trust in me.

Nikolai *opens the incubator.*

Do you want her to kill me instead?

Matty No.

Matty *stands up. He walks away from the nest.*

Nikolai *transfers the Grey Crane eggs. He closes the incubator.*

I wouldn't blame her if she did kill me.

A slight pause.

Nikolai If I tell her it was partly my fault. She will not kill
both of us.

Nikolai *stands up.*

We could say the Siberian eggs are the ones on the nest,
Matty?

A slight pause.

Matty What about those? You've just transferred them.

Nikolai I could put them back in the incubator? When
we return it would seem the same.

A pause.

Matty No.

A slight pause.

Well, unless you want to?

Nikolai My father would never forgive me if I lied to him.

Nikolai *offers his hand.*

If I shake your hand will you help me tell my father what has happened?

Matty *slowly walks to* **Nikolai**.

Nikolai *picks up the incubator.*

Matty I'll tell him, Nikolai.

The two boys shake hands.

Notes

These notes are intended for use by overseas students as well as by English-born readers.

5   *cobbled* – paved with rounded stones
5   *lace* – delicately woven cotton openwork
5   *Boots* – popular chain of chemists, now offering general goods
5   *Tsarist old Russia* – Pre-revolutionary Russia, ruled by the Tsars
5   *Vladimir Ilyich Lenin* – Bolshevik leader. First General Secretary of the Soviet Communist Party (lived 1870–1924)
6   *Wisconsin* – mid-Western state of the USA
6   *Siberia* – bleak North Eastern area of Russia
9   *make his year* – give him a thrill
9   *dotage* – enfeebled old age
9   *an old bugger* – colloquial term showing disrespect/old rogue
10   *gallivant* – to gad/move about furiously, irresponsibly
10   *the scapegoat* – the innocent one who is blamed
11   *rolling-pin treatment* – domestic retribution wielded by the woman of the house
12   *shenanigans* – misbehaviour with sexual connotations
14   *spanking new* – looking as new
14   *Enterprise* – a 14 foot sailing dinghy
14   *rugger* – rugby football
14   *nit* – silly person
14   *liberal* – tolerant
15   *well-heeled* – well-off financially
17   *hand-me-downs* – used clothes passed down to a younger child
17   *what we went through* – our experience of poverty

17   *toddler* – very young child
17   *The street didn't know* – the immediate neighbours
17   *if you had opposite sexes* – if your children were of opposite sex
17   *they kept it up* – continued to cross-dress
18   *transvestite* – person who dresses in clothes of the opposite sex
18   *the shoulder* – the person in whom neighbours confided their troubles
19   *you were early* – a premature baby
19   *can't do it* – i.e. assist with the birth
19   *the damp* – refers to the incessant moisture in the walls of the house
19   *stand-offish and snooty* – socially aloof
19   *common* – socially inferior, possibly with vulgar manners
19   *pinny* – pinafore – protective covering worn by women in the kitchen
20   *ten shilling note* – half the value of one pound before decimalisation but worth considerably more then than now
20   *put two 10ps on his eyes* – i.e. to keep them closed
21   *Scarborough* – coastal resort in Yorkshire .
21   *bairns* – Scottish and Northern English colloquialism for children
21   *skivvying* – doing menial domestic work
21   *scrat* – scavenge, scratch
21   *a sleeve on your doodah* – wear a condom
22   *apple in his eye* – his favourite (also 'apple of his eye')
23   *this way round* – Eileen is relieved that Jolyon died before her
24   *fall into bad company* – come under the influence of undesirables
27   *GP14 sailing dinghy* – General purpose 14 foot sailing dinghy
27   *a question and a half* – a difficult question
39   *palaver* – fuss
40   *hollered at* – shouted at

41   *three bags full* – refers to the end of the well-known nursery rhyme 'Baa baa black sheep' – Matty's sarcastic rebuff to Eileen's nagging

44   *ecology* – study of the interactions of animals and plants with each other and their environment

44   *Brukin Bor ... Pra River ... Oka nature reserve* – these are all to be found about 200 miles South of Moscow (*not* in Siberia)

45   *Hair in the gate* – refers to a hair endangering a film negative

46   *Royal Tunbridge Wells* – Kent town renowned for middle-class respectability

48   *ornithologist* – an expert in bird life

50   *p's and q's* – social niceties, literally referring to 'please' and 'thank you' / being on one's best behaviour

53   *good on them* – colloquial: good luck to them

54   *swot* – derogatory term for a hard-working student

54   *St Peter's School* – a long-established independent school in York

56   *Watt invented steam* – pun on the 18th Century James Watt, inventor of the steam engine

56   *heads above water* – survive financially

60   *Herculean* – extremely difficult, comparable to the labours of Hercules

62   *Young Pioneers* – Youth movement of the Communist Party

68   *May Day* – Socialist workers holiday held on May 1st

74   *bickered* – squabbled

79   *Quaker school* – School founded by the religious Society of Friends

80   *run to Brighton* – traditional outing by car

80   *Marxist* – follower of the philosophy of Karl Marx

81   *Teddy-boys* – youth group of the 1950's favouring quasi-Edwardian clothes – long jackets and narrow trousers

82   *Jerry Lee Lewis, Little Richard* – American rock 'n' roll singers

86 *scarf* – red scarf which symbolises the Young
     Pioneers (10–14 years old) the Konsomol (14–28
     years old) and the Communist Party Members in its
     three strands
89 *overstep the mark* – go too far
90 *a rocket will go up* – I'll lose my temper
99 *nurd* – a mildly abusive colloqualism implying
     stupidity
101 *dogsbody* – drudge, servant
101 *painter* – rope used to tie up a small boat
105 *Sony Walkman* – expensive personal stereo radio /
     cassette player
111 *Middlesborough* – large industrial town in Yorkshire
113 *pot egg* – artificial egg, used to deceive the mother
     bird

Methuen Student Editions

Methuen Modern Plays

include work by

Jean Anouilh
John Arden
Margaretta D'Arcy
Peter Barnes
Brendan Behan
Edward Bond
Bertolt Brecht
Howard Brenton
Simon Burke
Jim Cartwright
Caryl Churchill
Noël Coward
Sarah Daniels
Nick Dear
Shelagh Delaney
David Edgar
Dario Fo
Michael Frayn
John Guare
Peter Handke
Declan Hughes
Terry Johnson
Barrie Keefe

Stephen Lowe
Doug Lucie
John McGrath
David Mamet
Arthur Miller
Mtwa, Ngema & Simon
Tom Murphy
Peter Nichols
Joe Orton
Louise Page
Luigi Pirandello
Stephen Poliakoff
Franca Rame
Philip Ridley
David Rudkin
Willy Russell
Jean-Paul Sartre
Sam Shepard
Wole Soyinka
Theatre Workshop
Sue Townsend
Timberlake Wertenbaker
Victoria Wood

Methuen World Classics

Aeschylus (two volumes)
Jean Anouilh
John Arden
Arden & D'Arcy
Aristophanes (two volumes)
Aristophanes & Menander
Peter Barnes (two volumes)
Brendan Behan
Aphra Behn
Edward Bond (four volumes)
Bertolt Brecht
   (four volumes)
Howard Brenton
   (two volumes)
Büchner
Bulgakov
Calderón
Anton Chekhov
Caryl Churchill
   (two volumes)
Noël Coward (five volumes)
Sarah Daniels
Eduardo De Filippo
David Edgar
   (three volumes)
Euripides (three volumes)
Dario Fo (two volumes)
Michael Frayn
   (two volumes)
Max Frisch
Gorky
Harley Granville Barker
   (two volumes)

Henrik Ibsen (six volumes)
Lorca (three volumes)
David Mamet
Marivaux
Mustapha Matura
David Mercer (two volumes)
Arthur Miller
   (four volumes)
Anthony Minghella
Molière
Tom Murphy (three volumes)
Peter Nichols
   (two volumes)
Clifford Odets
Joe Orton
Louise Page
A. W. Pinero
Luigi Pirandello
Stephen Poliakoff
Terence Rattigan
Ntozake Shange
Sophocles (two volumes)
Wole Soyinka
David Storey
August Strindberg
   (three volumes)
J. M. Synge
Ramón del Valle-Inclán
Frank Wedekind
Oscar Wilde